THE OPTIMUM SOUL ENVIRONMENT
SHORT LIFE MOMENTS

By
Daniel G. Winklosky

**HIGH POINT, NORTH CAROLINA
NOVEMBER 24, 2001**

© 2003 by Daniel G. Winklosky. All rights reserved.

No part of this book may be reproduced, stored in a retrieval system, or transmitted by any means, electronic, mechanical, photocopying, recording, or otherwise, without written permission from the author.

ISBN: 0-7596-8448-0 (e-book)
ISBN: 0-7596-8449-9 (Paperback)

This book is printed on acid free paper.

1stBooks – rev. 10/07/03

ABOUT THE COVER SYMBOL

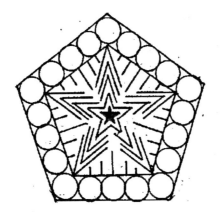

"5"
*** The Game the Angels Play***

*Depressed, sad, sorrowful, unhappy then play **"5"** the game the Angels play. Visualize yourself as the tiny star at the center of the symbolic shape. The circles around the band represent angels. Invite them to play **"5."** As they enter the game they will touch you, causing a tingle of pleasure. Then they will begin singing and sending love to you. Soon you will begin to feel uplifted, and begin even singing with them. In the meantime your starry shape grows larger and larger until it expands beyond the shape and you are singing and dancing with unbounded joy.* ***(Cover Symbol Design and Copyright by Daniel G. Winklosky)***

Peace be with you; for it is our responsibility to ourselves to have inner peace, from which we may extend a harmony to all about us! When loved ones depart, as in death, they are always in our spiritual awareness, awaiting for us to give them recognition, even our pets.... Life is beautiful, and must not be anything less, so reach for all that gives your heart the warmth and tingle of youthful innocence!

D. Taylor

See pages viii, 124, 131-138, 147, 163-165

PROLOG

Life is all about a series of events in some form of consciousness. The events are the mental and physical stimuli to our senses. This book is not going to flow from this page to the next or to the end. It isn't intended to, anymore than our lives do. Our thoughts are being constantly interrupted, as well as our physical pleasures. Sometimes these interruptions are joyful, but are usually just another momentary change in our experiences or thinking. This book reflects that in its composition. Every sentence is like another moment. It may be hard for the book to hold your attention. You will be challenged, you may read only a page or section a day, but you will discover the greater part of yourself.

It is the glancing, passing or fleeting moment that draws our attention. These are occurring continuously, moment by moment. Our lives are made up of these Short Life Moments, even if we are unaware of them. Every moment has meaning and adds to the wonder of our lives. Some moments are special like self-discovery, scenic pleasure, and ecstasy. Be alert and awake to as many "moments" as you can. Each of us lives life with some degree of awareness to these moments.

What we perceive from the physical senses such as hearing is dependent upon our sensitivity to sound. Equally important are the subtle and spiritual perceptions. We are usually less aware of these, but the unconscious part of us is recording them for us moment by moment. Whether physical or spiritual these moments are our guides to greater enjoyment of life.

The Short Life Moments that are life changing, transforming, or enlightening is not by accident. These are what I call "God" moments. Another term is "Zen" moment. For those who disdain god or religion, I'll call them "Moments of Creativity." The point is that we can awaken to the moments by training our sub-conscious to make us aware of the next transforming, delightful, and joyful moment.

Self-discovery through relationships is our purpose in life, and everyone is on a journey, which is what life is all about. These discoveries might be positive, like joy in what one accumulates in this life, and that is good. We accumulate negatives as well, like pain and that is bad. Avoid thinking of these negatives as forms of punishment, ill fortune or being a "victim" of circumstances. No one is really a "victim," because all experiences are both positive and negative, and in that context, being a "victim" is neither good nor bad. When life seems to be full of the negatives, our lesson is to accept them, acknowledge them, and learn from them. The paragraphs that follow highlight the special relationships and moments of my life.

> *Looking back, Dan is aware of how important the people who came into his life were, and how interesting they were in his life at just the right time. His older brother, Big Jack, was the best athlete, and during their growing up Dan was "pitted" against the best. Big Jack challenged him daily to stretch himself and develop his physical abilities, in order to compete one on one with Jack.*

> *Leaving high school and the Canal Zone was a dramatic step into the unknown, but few would know how determined Dan was to succeed and make his family proud. In college, he had an extraordinarily inspiring teacher for his architectural studies. Mr. George Winterowd taught design and history of architecture. Mr. Winterowd made positive comments on Dan's design abilities and transferred an enthusiasm and knowledge of architectural history to him.*

Following graduate school, Dan apprenticed with an architectural firm in New Orleans and later the Planning Department for the City of High Point in North Carolina. He began his own professional career, establishing the firm, Daniel G. Winklosky & Associates, in 1968. It was about this time that Mr. Gardner Gidley came into Dan's life as an associate, later partner, but always as his mentor.

While visiting in the Canal Zone, 1963, Kitty and Dan met, married within three months and later enjoyed growing older with two sons, Gary and Ward. The marriage lasted thirty years.

Dan's life seemed to flow freely, as if he were a spirit of the universe. His parents, younger sister, Mary Ann, and older brother Jack understood. Later his mentors would come to know that Dan was "not all there" and tried to keep part of him in touch with reality. Today, he looks forward to the future with confidence that there will appear in his life many new friends. Some of them will undoubtedly be mentors.

The expressed ideas and thoughts of the author have been significantly influenced by western philosophy, living abroad in the Canal Zone, being an American, and Protestant background. Though not absolute or concrete ideas and thoughts consist of truths. During the growing up process, truth changes, as does the level of spiritual awareness. Understanding increases as awareness rises through the 3rd through 7th dimensions of reality.

The artist interprets his subjects in visual form. The cover symbol and the sketches for the title pages of each part have expressed the artist in me. My artistic effort was easy and hopefully you appreciate and understand them. The author, like the artist, interprets his subject in a visual form of words and sentences, which the reader must interpret to find meaning and understanding. As author, my challenge is to convey the subject through a form of expression comprehensible to others. Giving expression to what I have experienced was not easy. Giving words to describe dreams and visions was even more difficult. The interpretation of those dreams and visions has been done with the hope that you will find pleasure reading this book.

Finding joy in life, seeing that life is beautiful, and knowing that every night the Creator whispers to us, "I shall always love you," was my lesson, which I now share with you.

THE OPTIMUM SOUL ENVIRONMENT
SHORT LIFE MOMENTS

CONTENTS

PROLOG v
INTRODUCTION xi
DRIP! DRIP! DRIP! THE WELL PLACED DRIP 1
PICK ME! PICK ME! 23
THE LIGHTS UPON THE HORIZON 83
EPILOG 123
APPENDIX OF ESSAYS 127

Dedicated To
Gary and Ward
And In Memoriam to the
WINKLOSKY FAMILY

INTRODUCTION

Most people are not asking for proof of God's existence, but an understanding of His Will and their service to that Will. Part of that service is to come before Him with joy and gladness.

There is a minimum of seven levels of awareness within the human being's experience of life. (See drawing in Appendix A, which illustrates these levels of awareness.) The Creator is Omni-present even in the single cell. There is intelligence in all things. Life is about awareness, your reality. This book presents in three parts those levels of awareness or dimensions of reality. The first part identifies the 1st and 2nd levels of awareness. The second part identifies the 3rd and 4th levels of awareness. The third part represents the concepts of awareness in the 5th, 6th and 7th dimensions of the human experience.

Smile! Smile and in that Moment you create an instantaneous Optimum Environment for your soul. We are body, mind, heart and spirit and the soul shares equally with each of them. When the body senses pleasure, the soul shares in that pleasure. When the heart experiences love the soul shares in that love. Whatever we create mentally or spiritually our soul enjoins in that creation, and it never forgets, nor does it judge us! Therefore, we should be about creating the **Optimum Soul Environment**, that is our individual purpose, whether for the body, or mind, or heart or spirit. It is our destiny, individually and collectively, to create the optimum soul environment. This book seeks to guide us in that effort, regardless of our circumstances.

As an architect, the author's desire is to create beautiful buildings. As a City Planner, the author's desire is to create beautiful environments. That should please the soul at the physical and mental levels, but it must please the soul at the emotional and spiritual levels, too. Bringing creativity to its highest form of expression can do that, but one must be convinced that such is a meaningful effort. One must believe there is an eternal soul and that there is a spirit abiding within each of us. This book seeks to awaken us to that possibility and then to acknowledge that reality.

We are all warriors, but where we differ is at the level of expression. Some of us are fist to fist warriors. Some others are mind to mind warriors. Others of us are heart to heart warriors, or spirit warriors. It is very frustrating for the heart warrior to convince the fist warrior to stop fighting. It is hard for the spirit warrior to convince the heart warrior to stop warring. This book seeks to raise the level of our consciousness to even higher levels of conscious understanding and behavior.

The beauty that is inherent in the earth and nature appeals to all of us at some moment in time. That same momentary delight can exist in our activities and our relationships. Those moments occur unexpectedly and delight us through body, mind, heart and spirit (through and through). This book seeks to identify those occasions, referring to them as "Life Moments" or **Zen Moments**, because of the impact they have upon our consciousness and our souls.

Each man may appear to have a beginning and ending, but is that our true reality? This book seeks to teach us that we are eternal light beings. The Light is without end and we are that Light! One will find some moment of pleasure while reading "The Optimum Soul Environment." Whatever it may be that says, "Yes!" one should ask what part of the soul was reached by the words or images and grow from there into the Light! That is the transformation. Allow the self, the individual, to become its true reality - a spark of Divine Love - and each soul will enjoy an optimum environment. When one sees a smile, one has seen the soul of another! Smile back, to the delight of both souls. Life is a gift, given to us by the Creator, that includes relationships with one another and with our self - body, mind, heart and spirit. (See Appendix B – Relationships and Individuality)

The Optimum Soul Environment is a book of **Short Life Moments** that challenge the difficult concepts of every day life by attempting to simplify the true meaning of life! Though this is a noble and difficult enough concept it is the reader who will determine if it has been attained. The seeds are sown. Some will react harshly, some will be skeptical, and some will ask questions to seek further understanding, growth and self-discovery.

What are the great moments of life called? How do you identify with the momentous ideas? Why do the great truths inspire us? How does the awareness between the conscious and higher conscious occur? Perhaps it's called a "Zen Moment." Several Zen Moments are provided. Any "Life Moment" that occurs to expand our awareness in a larger context within the Universe is a Zen Moment. It is hoped that some will find the concept that "seeing clearly" is an inspirational moment.

Everyone deals with "chaos" from their perception of reality, or their level of consciousness. There are those who do not understand themselves and are overwhelmed by the "chaos." I would hope this book is a ray of sunshine to bring them out of that hopelessness and to give them the assurance that life has purpose and meaning. Life is a gift. It is about relationships with the creator, with one another and with our self - body, mind, heart and spirit.

The titles of the three parts are *Drip, Drip, Drip (The Well Placed Drip)*, *Pick Me! Pick Me!* and *The Lights Upon the Horizon*. **Drip, Drip, Drip** is about the simple event of a drip. It asks the reader to acknowledge that if there is meaning in the universe, that the smallest drip has purpose! If the smallest drip has meaning, think how important and meaningful every moment of your life becomes. Putting ones attention upon a "drip" is a Zen Moment. It is the first level of awareness. This part prepares the reader for **Pick Me! Pick Me!** This is about kickball at a time of youthful exuberance, when the real purpose of that period of a kid's life was to play! This is the third level of awareness. The reader is then exposed to the meaning of "light" in the last story, which is about the fifth and six levels of awareness. **The Lights Upon the Horizon** is about what makes living a special event. It is about creating a philosophy of life as a way of living. Some text is taken from essays that are provided in the Appendix.

It is hoped that the three parts of Short Life Moments provided herein will be enlightening. A major part of writing them was in the pleasure, moment by moment. Readers may find them creative, historical and maybe even humorous, but hopefully inspirational.

The Optimum Soul Environment

DRIP! DRIP! DRIP!

THE WELL PLACED DRIP

DANIEL GOEHRING
WINKLOSKY

HIGH POINT, NORTH CAROLINA
APRIL 15, 2001

Daniel G. Winklosky

Dedicated to
Mary Ann, Jack, Mom and Dad
Majaddam

The Optimum Soul Environment

DRIP! DRIP! DRIP!

THE WELL PLACED DRIP

CONTENTS

```
PREFACE ............................................................. 5
CHAPTER 1  –  HOW DRIPS ARE BORN ......................... 8
CHAPTER 2  –  WHEN THE DRIPS ARE DOWN ............ 13
CHAPTER 3  –  DRIPS, DRIPS AND NOTHING BUT
                DRIPS! ................................................ 18
APPENDIX C – ANALYSIS OF A COFFEE DRIP
                A RESOURCE ..................................... 139
APPENDIX D – EVERYONE IS A SPARK OF DIVINE
                LOVE ................................................. 143
```

Daniel G. Winklosky

PREFACE

If one can accept that the Universe is purposeful, then it would be true to state that every action and reaction in the galaxy is ordained. It would suggest that every result on the planet is meaningful. Likewise, every life is a part of a larger plan, and any seemingly insignificant act, like a drip, is well directed and perfectly placed.

Finding the creative power in a drip that is capable of changing the physical environment through "erosion" is a very highly spiritual concept, occurring mostly in the eastern religious philosophies, especially in the Japanese gardens.

There is no duality of meaning or demeaning of life anywhere, throughout the following chapters. Perhaps the attempts at humor are less successful than the intention, but do not associate the "drip" with any reference or irreverence to life or people.

Drips come in all colors, sizes, shapes, and sayings. After every drip is another well placed drip. Remember the saying, "A drip by any other name is still a drip." Bad drips drive out good drips. A drip in the wind is worth two in the hand. Drip on others, as you would have them drip on you. The legends of drips are certainly worth noting. The major sayings prevalent in the lore and customs of generations are worth noting in regard to their drip implications.

Re-write all the cliches, typos, sayings, maxims and laws you know or can remember in **drip form** and witness a cultural **drip shift**. Given how fluid life's experiences are, there will be a surprised shift of consciousness towards the drip. This would elevate the joy of anticipating life, living each day to enjoy the moment of every drip that drops upon us.

The most popular drip is something that a nationwide poll should decide. There is no telling how many choices there are. It would be nice to obtain examples of the most humorous drip, the ugliest drip, the most embarrassing drip, the most colorful, natural, etc., types of known drips. *I'll be happy to begin documenting the drip experiences the world over. If you have a drip anecdote to spare or share, send it along to me.*

If the first drip didn't get your attention; nor the second drip, then the third drip surely did. That's how it happened to me. This whole thing on drips started while I was seated on an airplane, returning to the United States. Prior to landing, water accumulated above me somehow. There were three drips and zoom, I unbuckled and jumped out of my seat all in one motion! There were more beads of water on the storage compartment above the seat. The flight attendant apologized. She said it was the fault of the airplane and applied a bandage (napkin and tape) to the source! Why? How come it was only on my seat that it dripped? Where did the drips come from, or were they prophetic teardrops? What was I to understand from this event? Who was giving me the basis for an innovative story about drips?

Another question to consider is, "How much influence does a small event have upon one's life," even if one acknowledges these 'trivial' events? I do not believe anything to be uneventful, and having said that, I do not know how to give meaning to every little event. (See Analysis of a Drip in Appendix C)

I am reminded of the philosophy of Soren Kierkegaard on choices, and how agonizingly painful life is to have to consider all the ramifications of one's decisions. I do feel that whatever choices we make, it's OK, as long as we acknowledge full responsibility for them. Choices put each of us upon the journey of life and acknowledging responsibility is the path toward understanding and awareness. What we choose to see and accept as meaningful is the part of the journey we enjoy and that we relate too emotionally. Making the journey fun is the key. The intent of these chapters is to provide a basis for the freedom to believe that and to have fun living life like that. So, have fun, the journey of a drip is presented to you for the rest of your life.

I know the Creator has a great sense of humor, and that joy is his gift to all. Remember to laugh when the next drip hits you, and the universe will laugh with you. Complain and you still look funny, so the universe will again laugh at you, as well as your friends. So if you are a witness to or recipient of that, oh, so well placed drip, just smile!

Daniel G. Winklosky

CHAPTER 1 - HOW DRIPS ARE BORN

The United States is not a civilization of splurgers, streamers, gushers, all or nothing kinds of people. Instead the American people are patient, economical, thrifty, kind, and are attracted to the slow, methodical, timely placed drip. Nothing drips like success! More importantly, the drip is the cornerstone of our economy. Recall the "Trickle Down" economic theory, which is still a "drip economy" by any other name.

A drip has to have certain physical properties before it is a drip, as well as for when it is no longer called a drip. The drip becomes an independent entity when it releases from the larger source, and is falling or flying free of all effects, except gravity and the Creator. It's not the size of the drip that counts. It is the fact that a drip is individualized and in a free fall. This freedom to be gives the drip its character. The drip leaves the source quietly, then free falls to create an impact, landing upon some material object, such as a car windshield. The impact creates a sound, which is defined by the size, speed and the material object impinged upon. There is a great variety just in the intensity of the sound. The drip is born, when it leaves the source. The drip begins as a "tear drop shape," suggesting that drips have emotions. The drip is sad, as it parts from its source. But the drip continues its free fall, growing into a perfect sphere. This sphere is capable of expressing any one of the colors of the rainbow as it falls. There is a guiding will as surely as there is a well placed drip.

The essence of the Creator always remains, regardless of the shape, place or make-up of the drip. During its short lifetime, the drip experiences a wide range of events. The most impressive events are its "splats." Splats are not to be confused with splashes, because those are a bunch of drips doing their individual splats all at once. Splash! See? Being a drip always has its moments, too. It is hard for a drip to be dripped on, but it is theoretically possible, during free fall. That would be like being "soul mates" in human terms. Humans have no way of knowing about the drips except through eye contact and observation. I like drips, and haven't met a drip I didn't like. Of course anyone can get upset about some drips, but at my age, there is a lot more patience and understanding toward them. After all, they are so short lived, it is important to forgive those unpleasant ones on the rare occasions when they caused embarrassment or displeasure. Remember all the drips that left with our fond memories of them. I've observed how some are influenced by drips. There is the whole gamut of reactions – some funny, some tickled, sad, relief, accidental, surprised, but always colorful.

The personal drip is what is most common to all humans, such as the "drippy nose." I've had hay-fever all my life, so drips and torrents have poured forth from these nostrils, unabated at times, many times. This brings up the premature burial of a drip, blowing one's nose or wiping sweat from the brow. The potential of every drip should be honored and blowing noses or wiping sweat should be against the law. I say this with one Kleenex tissue at hand, because I've found that if the nose is not blown it will become "stuffed" and the drips will just start falling from the eyes, thereby becoming teardrops. The ability of the body to release drips is uncanny, beyond the scope of this book too. I have many spots on my ties to identify how hard drips try! I could have eaten that whole spoonful of soup, but no, a wayward drip had to make a splat. The problem here is that drip see, drip do! Other drips of soup soon splattered and splashed over the areas of my tie. I bury my ties, and all the brother and sister drips with it. Maybe that's wise or maybe it should be burned. I truly don't know of any correct protocol on this matter.

When the drip finally comes to the end of its time, as a splat, it is important to notice that its fluidity disappears, vanishes, possibly ascending into heaven? This is true! The color may remain but the drip ascends or evaporates into the ethers back to the Creator. It's almost too human, isn't it? But feel good about the passing drip. It's now in a better place free of its physical self. Let me hasten to state that anyone might still hear that drip during dreams and know that all is well with it in its new place of being. There are no nationalities of drips, but there are drip cultures. Yet for all their seeming differences they are all alike in their physical characteristics. A drip drips and splats, every single one of them.

I am a little squeamish about some drips. When I see a drip of blood, I turn off the TV. That's not a comfort zone for me, so when it's my blood that's dripping away from a cut or anything else that caused the bleeding I want it back! That's my first thought. By the time I see blood though it's too late. The wisest thing for me to do next is to prevent any more drips from leaving me, block the door so to speak. First aid, as it applies to blood, is the result of teaching that the human body has only so much blood and no more. Therefore, applying pressure to the points of the body where the drip occurred must stop any drips of blood. This technique is known as a Band-Aid application. A much larger problem would require an application of a tourniquet, which is placed at an important juncture of arteries in that part of the body where the blood is dripping. The problem with this last method is that the individual surrenders all the drips not controlled by the tourniquet. Knowing that the human condition is dependent upon the blood system circulating throughout the body, it is a challenge to make sure the blood contains all the best qualities to promote good health and longevity. This includes the ability of the blood to clot or cease dripping. The blood can do this. Isn't it amazing! There is a fine line between blood letting and taking blood. I don't even want to write any further about dripping blood, because I know a lot of others feel the same way I do.

The past, present and future of a drip is so unpredictable. The most historical drip was discovered by the kid in Holland, when he put his finger in the dike, preventing more drips which might have flooded a lot of families. The kid that put his finger in the dike must have had hay-fever or allergies as a tyke, so that putting his finger in the dike was not a whole lot different from a tyke putting his finger in a nostril to stop the drips. The most disastrous drip is the bird doo! Yuk! No more be said about that other than that it doesn't happen to the rich. The most popular drip is the kitchen sink. The most frustrating drip is the one coming from the ceiling, which I've noticed frustrates both the plumber and roofer.

Do drips multiply? Yes they do! Gestation varies widely. Upon observation of life's drips and drops, it seems clear to me that they will always exist. Perhaps, taking an appreciative position for their existence, one can accept them and go on to live a more productive life. Those who would consider a glass as being half full are being optimistic and would tend to view a drop as a drip, and dark cloudy skies as a potentially drippy day. This optimism has very little scientific basis, but humanity, being what it is, is characteristically hopeful. If one believes that the clouds will begin to drip, then it is a very good probability that they will drip, making one a better prognosticator than the weatherman, who is right half the time.

When a drip is born, it's on its way, and it's mostly down hill from there. There are the occasional drips that get caught in an upward movement. If those upward movements are accompanied by cold air, then the drip becomes a hail stone after which it hits the ground hard, then melts. For a drip to become a hailstone is a drip type of honor. The cold associated with the process of becoming a hailstone is severe. It may require several earthward trips and then upward climbs, accumulating other drips (like rolling a snowball). Drips can accumulate sufficiently to grow to the size of dimes, quarters and grapefruits. I've never seen them the size of grapefruits, just read or heard about them. A frozen drip has to be a hailstone or a **snowflake**. My idea of a drip is going to be different than another's idea; but I would hope everyone could be at peace with these different philosophies about drips.

Daniel G. Winklosky

Politics can definitely enter into the life of a drip. One man, one drip! And that goes for all the women and children too! Can you imagine a case where a drip missed? Would the Creator call for a mulligan? No! The heavenly source of drips is proof of this. Even if evil existed, it cannot initiate drips. All drips are born of goodness. If there is a drip that misses, I feel it is due to the use of free will inherent in the drip, "drippee," "overseer" of the situation, or some other observer, which could be an angel. Angels exist! Prove to me they don't! Thank your lucky drips for them. Truly, having **little** faith in the goodness of drips is going to be a lifetime handicap.

CHAPTER 2 - WHEN THE DRIPS ARE DOWN

Sometimes the falling drips, in combinations, perform a musical score, delighting the ears and senses of the listener to hear dibble, dibble, dop, dop! When repeated over the period of an hour, the listener can be entranced and float into another world, much like meditation. If, on the other hand, the drip, in combinations, becomes boring and causes the listener to feel edgy, dripped on, or uncomfortable then this is known as the Chinese water torture.

There are the very slow drips. So slow that Americans developed a saying "slow as molasses," applicable to some human behavior. The drip from a spoonful of honey, almost empty syrup bottles, or molasses jar gets credit for that statement. Other drip forms may be slower because of the weather. It seems almost certain that a drip in the far north will freeze, which is called a snowflake or icicle, whereas, a drip in the equatorial south will be regarded as perspiration. Perspiration is another human body fluid, which I'm not as concerned about as blood, but there is a certain disagreeable odor to that drip, which is only trying to cool down the body. This disagreeable odor does not leave the object (like a shirt), when the spirit fluid evaporates. I use deodorants, or powders, such as talc to slow or eliminate the drip of perspiration. If the source of the drip is the head of a person, one might note the wearing of a bandana or hat to stifle the drip. Other body functions serve to create drip conditions. But what can anyone really expect, as earthlings? This is a fluid planet with water over two-thirds of its surface area and a fiery core, like a star, which is why some call it the Blue Star planet. Given these facts it cannot be too much to expect that the drip is almost as old as the earth.

In the northern climes the icicles melt, creating white looking drips, but if the sun is shining and in the right position these drips are colorful (violet, red, orange, yellow, green, blue). At night the drips are black! The drips of the east and west are associated largely with rainfall and oceans. Water runoff of the rainfall begins from the mountains to the rivers then to the oceans. Swimmers know the experience of being dripping wet; because they either have to towel dry or drip dry in the sun. How does it feel when the unexpected drip hits one in the face? A snowflake has the same effect and it too is a drip from heaven. No one should be called a drip (noun), but anyone may be referred to as dripping (adjective). The most often referenced "dripping" is the one of "name dropping;" it's a dripping!

One of my not so favorite drips occurs while I'm in the bathtub, soaking up the warm water. It's the cold drip that splats on my neck. Remember it? That's what I'm talking about. The source of that drip is from the underwear drying on hangers above me. A shower person must have been the designer responsible for clothes made to "drip dry." When that happened, I too had to start taking showers.

If one has a spiritual awakening, it will come in drips and drabs, which is called spiritual enlightenment. Nirvana does not come easy; it is fraught with tests of one's knowledge and application of wisdom, which is where most everyone fails at one time or another. Finding a path to the greater self can be accomplished by studying and observing the lowly drip. I am invoking a "**Zen Moment**." If one can put one's self in the place of a drip, one will find their special self. Just because one experiences the "splat" while in this meditation, note that the fluidity of the drip is beginning to evaporate. It is becoming another essence of itself in another place. If the "splat" is only a momentary event, the drip may reform and fall again, incorporating life after "splat death."

From a scientific perspective the drip is a molecular structure of many atoms of the major elements composing it. In a physical sense, when the drip is a water molecule and falls as

The Optimum Soul Environment

rain, it is a sphere of hydrogen and oxygen or two gasses. If that same drip is at a much higher altitude, it is no longer a sphere of water, but a water balloon, a bubble of water, found in situations where you have mists or clouds. This is true! Another scientific observation about drips is that they occur in the mornings of cold days as "dew!" Furthermore, meteorites and comets are cosmic molecules, which, on entering the earth's atmosphere, become "cosmic drips," because they melt, drip, evaporate or "splat."

The most exceptional or miraculous drip is as "manna" from heaven. Another notable and miraculous drip is referred to as the "nectar" of the Gods. Of course these are the ancient phrases and may be how the languages of the olden days referred to their drips. Of course, they may not be too different from our own modern drips of "nectar and manna."

Another ancient story or tale is the one about "Chicken Little." The name itself implies the naivete of this chick that felt a drop from heaven and ran off half cocked saying, "The sky is falling! The sky is falling!" This little chick was presenting a moral: Don't take all one experiences at face value and don't believe everything one hears. Good advice! But the sky was falling! It was raining! Another truism is that drips fall down *most of the time.*

This brings up the point of making a career out of drips. These professionals are called plumbers, because they have to deal with drips all the time, everyday throughout their careers. Plumbers have to be careful because the whole family of a drip can go whoosh, all at once for a long time. Plumbers also have to deal with two types of drips - the hot ones and the cold ones.

There was, sad to say, a time in the 50's that some individuals were called drips. These unfortunate souls were a thing of the 50's, because all individuals were given some kind of nasty name like four eyes (if you wore glasses), panty waste (if a guy was scared), and lardo (if one were too heavy). It was hard to be acceptably human, so a lot of young people were called "drips" back then. In the later decades of the 60's and 70's these same types of people that were referred to as drips in the past, became known as "kooks" and "nerds."

Hasn't everyone run up to the back of someone and tapped them on the shoulder? But then they turned around and it wasn't who one thought it was, actually someone else or a total stranger, perhaps. But the look in their eye said it all. "What are you?" Some kind of drip? Some kind of kook? No, today they are just being blunt and bold enough to say what's what. Among all the problems of society and the world, mistaken identities cannot be high on the list of bad things. It's certainly not as bad as a limp handshake.

Now, the dog is man's best friend because he barks and protects the family, home, and territory. Does anyone know why he barks? Its because he has spent every day several times a day "marking" out the territory he calls his. It's a doggy thing. This "marking" technique is great for outdoors, so an invading dog or person gets barked at. When "marking" is a happening inside, those indoor drips are not OK, are they?

When the drip hits the fan, there are all kinds of possibilities, resulting from the events. First, there's always the sound. It goes ping rather than splat, and the drip can be whipped out. It may fly past, but most drips that hit the fan still go ping or splat and vanish back into thin air. Depending upon the surface object, splats have special sounds. Think about these materials and try to imagine the drip hitting upon marble, porcelain, tin, wood, paper, carpet, raincoat, umbrella, and leaves, to name a few. If one has a discerning ear for sound, notice there is a significant difference between a tin splat and a carpet splat. I believe the great musicians took inspiration from these movements to create their own on paper.

Another one of my favorite forms of a drip is the coffee maker in the morning. I can hear the drip before I smell the

The Optimum Soul Environment

coffee, and when I hear that first drip, I begin a process called salivating, as my own body generates liquids that proceed to the mouth and occasionally drip out. This is the ultimate human conditioning. By a drip! Imagine that! A drip has that much control over the human body functions. If one hasn't had a drip-dried cup of coffee, what have they missed? Well, there are other human bodily functions, too, that are the cause for more drips.

The values of well-placed drips are lessons in humility, appreciation, responsibility and serenity; among others. Everyone has felt the drip of humility and tasted the drip of pleasure. Drips are part and parcel of each and every day and occur all year round.

Daniel G. Winklosky

CHAPTER 3 - DRIPS, DRIPS AND NOTHING BUT DRIPS!

As far as the eye can see, it's raining!

A state of being unconscious is about not knowing one was hit by a drip, didn't see it coming, where it came from, or how it felt. It is a very real responsibility for the world's populations to be aware of drips and the how, when, where, what and why of them. No kidding! Do not oversimplify any drip or its location. The spiritual essence of the drip must be acknowledged as well as its source and pathway. There is surely a metaphysical meaning in its presence. It would not exist if it were otherwise.

Standing next to the car, one heard "splat!" Looking under the car one saw a black spot. It looked like oil, it smelled like oil, and it tasted like oil. Now one must consider the source for this oil drip. Isn't it fair to assume one would be concerned about where the source of this oil drip is? I think so, case in point. If I had not been beside the car, the "splat" of the drip would not have been heard to alert me to getting its source checked. Even had I missed the sound of the "splat," the evaporated oil spot would convey a similar message to my eyes.

None could survive without the drips. When rainfall is plentiful, there is an abundance of foods, which translates into health and long life. If there is consistent draught, or lack of drips, over a sufficient period of time, this translates into food scarcity, ill health and a shorter life. Rainfall is measured in a tiny cylinder that is able to catch each drip of falling rain. One drip is a trace. A larger number of drips can measure a couple of inches, or more! Heavenly drips are our most important commodity and rank second only to the air we breath. Incidentally, the air is made more palatable because it has drips of water, referred to as humidity. A hundred percent humidity reading is rain or heavy fog, which is sure to drip!

The Optimum Soul Environment

Each week is filled with forecasters giving the odds on drip days. A more effective and meaningful forecast would be the approximate number of drips. A thousand drips per second might be a torrential rain, ten drips per second might be a light rain shower or fog. Twenty percent of the news is consumed by the question is it or isn't it going to drip? Does it matter? No! I wrote earlier that every drip was precisely timed, and more importantly, accurately aimed by its Creator, the Rain God! The rain dances of the elders were not so idly laughable as previously thought, are they? I remember a great saying, "Don't let the drips get in your eyes." The words of that old saying had a meaning and could be visually and audibly appreciated. Looking up into the rain is not a good idea. The only time to look up is to get an eye "drip" for dry eyes or pink eyes. One can get any number of medical drip dosages through the eyedroppers (eyedrippers). The medical technological advancements hit their peak with the IV, a drip method of dosing. Self-directed IV's mean that the patient can control the rate of the drips. For those who are in a situation of pain, these self-dosed drips are a Godsend. Perhaps the most important of these IV drips is the cancer patient's self-induced dosing of morphine, or any similar drug. The cancer abating and other medical IV drips raises man's technical ability to the highest level of human care.

No chapter about drips can be complete until one considers the implications of a world without drips. OK? I believe that says it all. A world without drips is no world at all, at least not an earthly physical world like I know.

The legends of drip, drips, dripping, drippy, and dripped have yet to be historically documented. What has been documented is that life, throughout the millenniums, established their existence by their residue. It seems that when the earth withdraws water and applies heat a special substance is created. Deep ground deposits of oil, thick, sticky goo came into existence and another presence within the earth is coal.

Daniel G. Winklosky

What has this to do with drips? We've already stated that drips evaporate and leave only their residue.

When the initial drips that occur from rain hit the extremely hot pavement, the heat of the pavement causes them to evaporate before or immediately upon hitting. The rains that have their drips falling, when the sun is shining, become known as sun showers. But these drips turn quickly into a mist and evaporate in the heat of the sunshine. It is as though one ray of sunshine lights up one drip, causing it to be in a sort of spotlight, and after its moment of fame, the drip is gone. Babies are just great sources of drips. The loss of a child is sad. Does the Creator put the spirit of that child into a ray of light? What if all departed spirits were reflected rays of sunlight from a drip!

Another beautiful dripping is associated with a pool of water. Ripples or rings are created from the rain falling in drops. Here the splat changes to plop. A lot of drips can create a sing song melody – dibble, dibble, dop, dop. Listen carefully, while walking in the rain to hear how each drip sounds and whether there is a message in the sound of the drips.

"Dripped on" leads to many types of "accidents," some are gross, some funny, and some are hardly worth writing about, but all are important. Isn't it ironic that a drip on a woman's nice dress ruins the whole evening for her, and that a stained shirt has to have another drip to take it out, like "Spray and Wash?"

There is always some type of drip in your life every day. The only ones I am truly aware of are the outlandish occasions in which they occur. While in Milan in front of the Cathedral, I was sketching the structure until a huge greenish drip "splattered" on the drawing. Naturally, I threw the sketch away, jumped up and looked around in amazement, because nobody else had seen this pigeon induced drip event.

Most encounters with a drip are very personal, like one on one. On the other hand, if one remembers how to make a home made milkshake, use ice cream, milk and stir well. Sometimes there is a mass of ice-cream foam on top, blocking the milkier part of the milkshake. Remember how it takes a while for the milk to work its way through the heavier cream floating on top? If one is not careful the whole glob of the foam can plunge forward and hits nose and face followed by the milkier part of the shake, which flows out and down the chin, and drips onto the lap. This has happened.

I made such a milkshake for my Dad. My Dad began drinking the milkshake. Anticipating the pleasure of it, he said, "Ah!" He kept tipping the glassful of milkshake, but nothing was coming out. Finally, it burst forth all over him! He laughed! The whole front of him was dripping of milkshake. I learned a major lesson that day; to laugh when there is nothing else to do, because of a drip. Thanks, Dad!

After a rainstorm, while the trees are still leafless, the beads of water all over the tree are holding the potential of a drip. Studying the visual landscape for the moment of a drip is quietly beautiful and relaxing. Watching a bead of water roll across a leaf and come to a stop at the edge, "Should I or shouldn't I," seems to be the question on the potential for that drip. Studying one's reflection in a pond of water is a moment of note. Then, amazingly, to see one's image dissolve in the ringlets created by a drip. This awareness of life's fluid moments has no end.

The wonderful reflections that everyone has of their lives are the keys and means to be even more alert to life, even to the smallest drip. For as surely, as the Creator made little green apples, he made drips first!

There is an event referred to as seeing the white light by individuals in near death situations, as well as others I'm sure. This event might be the concept of the "collective ancestral spirits," the "Holy Ghost," or more aptly the "Holy Host." That glowing white light is Unconditional Love. It is incorporated within every soul. We are individualized light sparks of Divine Love. The Holy Host are our relatives and friends, who may choose to reveal themselves to us, as spirit. Everyone is a spark of **Divine Love**. (See Drawing, which illustrates this in Appendix D.).

The wave of **Divine Love** enters one's life. **Divine Love** gives rise to life. If Divine Love were withdrawn and since all life is spirit then life would be withdrawn instantaneously, leaving the body to return to dust. The unseen **Psychic** and **Cosmic Properties** are the undetected Light and magnetic qualities of the ethereal universe, which give an immeasurable, but additional mass to the atomic weights of all the elements and adds substance and influence to our thoughts and actions. **Impressions** are the thoughts of the individual mind, and humanity's collective mind, which will manifest as actions and deeds in the reality of the earth plane.

Without **air** life can be sustained for a few minutes, without **water** life can be sustained for a few days, and without **food** life can be sustained for a few months. This is true of our earthly reality unless **Divine Love** intercedes to extend life, altering the Laws of Earth, as we know them to be.

From the separation of God through despair up to the importuning - "God, if there is a God" - God's Love becomes realized and the spirit of the individual is resurrected. Life, once again, has meaning and purpose and the soul rejoices. Despair evaporates into the false reality that it represents and is no more!

So, the threats to life are reversible. The chaos that clutters the world has purpose, but in a spiritual sense is an illusion. Only the truth of Divine Love is real. But the earth plane is the realm of three dimensions, of dualities, and of human experiences. All are to learn to live in this world, and to create a new heaven on earth, making it an ideal place for all to dwell.

The Optimum Soul Environment

PICK ME! PICK ME!

DANNY WINLOSKY

PUSAN, SOUTH KOREA
DECEMBER 25, 2000

Daniel G. Winklosky

In Memoriam
**Jack, My Older Brother, A Big Kid, too!
Mary Ann, My Younger Sister, A Princess!
Mom and Dad, My Parents, MAJADDAM!**

The Optimum Soul Environment

PICK ME! PICK ME!

CONTENTS

PREFACE... 27
CHAPTER 1 – KICKBALL... 29
CHAPTER 2 – WORKUPS 39
CHAPTER 3 – TEAMS.. 48
CHAPTER 4 – PICK ME! PICK ME! 56
CHAPTER 5 – THE LEGENDS................................. 71
APPENDIX E – CANAL ZONE
                   GLOSSARY OF PROPER NAMES AND
                   TOPICS FOR FURTHER INTEREST...... 146
APPENDIX F – THE JOY OF FREEDOM 151
APPENDIX G – ZEN STRING
                   AN ALTERNATIVE RACQUETBALL
                   GAME 154

Daniel G. Winklosky

PREFACE

How much influence should parents have in the growing up of their children? Personally, it is my belief that the children will take care of themselves, during their free playtime. Their growing up, though, must be monitored, because there will need to be a safety net to prevent them from getting into "deep waters." An observant society or neighborhood can do this. That was the manner of the neighborhood reality I was aware of during my youth.

My sons, Gary and Ward, have been a constant pleasure. Their growing up was no easier than mine or yours, so I am proud and appreciative of their individual accomplishments. Our paths have parted, many times, but it is important to me that all the ties and bonds between us be remembered, renewed when possible, but always cherished.

This part can hardly be understood without some reference to how it began as a work of enjoyment. It was as though all the conditions for writing it fell into place at one time, without any form of distraction. It began as a series of hand written ideas or notes, about the past in the Canal Zone. That was a time of remembering how much fun I associated with those youthful days, and how memorable they were on a day to day basis. No different than anyone else's life to be sure, but it was a childhood innocence at its best. As the writing progressed the experience of writing took on a magical quality all of its own. The ballpoint pen never faltered, or skipped, providing total control over the paper, and, perhaps me! It was completed before I realized what I had done in three days, over Christmas in Pusan, Korea. This is my Christmas gift to those youths, and I hope others who can share the same pleasure in remembering when it was all so much fun just to be a kid.

Daniel G. Winklosky

Congratulations to all who have maintained their kickball values over all these years, especially if over thirty, or reclaimed them, as an over sixty type of person in this, the latter part of life. A special thanks to Judy, Becky, Ritchie, Pat, Cheena, Helen, Timmy, Jimmy, Eddie, John and the many others that have been true friends, making my growing up a lot easier. It is more important to thank you now than never at all, but I suspect you've known all these years how much I cared for each of you!

The subject is kickball. The setting is the Canal Zone in Panama. The description and accounts of the Canal Zone are shown in Italics.

CHAPTER 1 – KICKBALL
This is the first of five chapters.

The history of the Panama Canal and Canal Zone began with the French Canal Commission. The president of that commission and the engineer in charge was Ferdinand De Lessseps. It was his engineering genius that completed the building of the Suez Canal in Egypt. His miscalculation of costs and malaria in Panama contributed to his inability to build the canal across the Isthmus of Panama. Theodore Roosevelt's efforts to take on the construction of the Canal began with the revolt of the Panamanians from Colombia. In 1903, the Panama Canal Commission was established. The Commission purchased the rights and assets of the French Canal Commission and then purchased all the land within a ten-mile width and 50 mile length of the proposed route of the Canal. Deeds of these land parcels exist. I've seen them!

In my neighborhood, when I was growing up, we played **kickball**. We played all day long; we may have broken for lunch, but had to break for dinner. Since everyone didn't eat dinner at the same time, you could always eat fast and get back to play in a game of "**workups**."

These first few sentences are already creating trouble for my readers; I'd be surprised if it didn't! Kickball; no let's start with my neighborhood! I grew up in the town of "**Diablo Heights**." The population of "Diablo," as we called it, was about 5,000. I think that included **big dogs**, and there were a lot of them. (That's another interesting topic and is explained later.) The neighborhood was called "**Davis Street**," which meant all the kids, dogs and parents were included, but not cats, since they didn't play kickball or any sport for that matter. **Big dogs** played kickball.

Daniel G. Winklosky

Many communities were built to serve the locks on the Pacific and Atlantic sides of the Canal. These communities were job specific to the locks or to the administration and service of it. In addition to these civilian communities, there were military bases constructed for all branches (airforce, marines, navy and army). Diablo Heights (like Balboa, Ancon, Pedro Miguel, and Gamboa) was one of the towns that were built on the Pacific side of the "**Canal Zone**." Diablo still exists as a town today. Administrators changed the name of the Canal Zone (**CZ**) to the Panama Canal Zone and got away with it. The administrators tried to change the name of Diablo Heights to "Altos de Jesus." It never caught on, and it's still called Diablo! But that's politics, and has no place in this chapter or any of the following chapters.

Unlike most city streets one would be familiar with, Davis Street had small spaces between 4-family houses. Five 4-families down each side of Davis Street at that time comprised the neighborhood. These small spaces provided for an excellent kickball milieu.

Now, kickball is a sport. It was once more popular than it is today. There were kickball **teams**, kickball tournaments, and champions. Being on a championship kickball team was worth something in those days. One played kickball as if one were starting out to play baseball. I use this analogy only because everyone is more familiar with it. It's ironic that kickball existed before baseball. There was a catcher, pitcher and all the basemen, shortstop, and outfielders. That's the end of the similarity, but that's not quite true. I don't have a kickball rule book, and I never knew if a rulebook on kickball ever existed. Honestly! One could tell if someone was "making up a rule," because it was usually in their favor or their team's favor.

Kickball was played like baseball, but not quite. The ball was much larger, so large one had to inflate it with air. A well-inflated ball was most important to the game, but rarely such good fortune happened, as all the balls "leaked." One could tell by the smell. Remember how car tire inner tubes smell when the air comes out? That's what I smelled when a ball had a leak. (Fixing a kickball is like fixing a bicycle inner tube and must be explained later in the chapter.) Back to kickball, I've explained the neighborhood, haven't I?

The pitcher rolls the ball to the "batter" in which case it is not appropriate here, because the ball is being rolled to the "kicker." Get it! Kickball! The term "rolling" the ball to the kicker is correct. A wily pitcher, though, has many deliveries. These are made underhanded, although I think sidearm and overhand were used, because I seem to remember we used them. That may have been a "rules" observation. One can get away with a rules observation if one is bigger than any one else or had a team that would back up this rule.

There is a home plate. If there are not enough players, the "kicking" team provides the catcher. This is because the ball has to be thrown back to the pitcher. Only tournaments had umpires. Otherwise, it was pretty obvious to the pitcher and catcher if the ball passed across the plate, or any part of it. Calling balls and strikes (like in baseball) resulted in a walk with four balls, or a strike out with three strikes. Kicking out at a kickball and missing it is a strike, but its more embarrassing though than swinging at and missing a baseball. Watching a kicker miss the ball was always hilarious, if one were in the field. If the kicker was a teammate, I pretended not to see it, turning to look into the sky, with a sort of bemused look.

Another bemusing story is the fact that the sun rises on the Pacific Side a few minutes before it does on the Atlantic Side of the Panama Canal. It is an anomaly of geography and many a bet was made and won with this knowledge, especially by families returning to the States on vacations. The reason for this is that the Canal is going northwest to southeast, putting the Pacific terminus further east than the Atlantic terminus. Great! Right?

So far one must think he could have even played kickball, and with a confidence of being quite good or successful at it. But let me say, it is a game that requires great ability, flexibility, dexterity, and agility.

Pitching a kickball is a special talent, much harder than both cricket and baseball put together. One can deliver the ball smoothly along the ground straight to the plate and get kicked in the face by the ball, which hurts, a lot! So, to prevent this type of hurt, the pitcher holds the ball in the palm of the hand, with the fingers and arm, giving control. Now when the windup takes the arm above the shoulder, the ball is securely held. The downswing provides the force. The pitcher can still deliver the ball smoothly along the ground, but at a much greater velocity. True, he still might get the ball kicked back toward his face. It would be coming faster too! It is with this added awareness that the pitcher can make a delivery by twisting the wrist to give the ball a "wicked" curving delivery to the kicker. This technique probably accounts for all the successful bowlers, like Ronnie and Timmy. The "break" of the ball into its curve may occur immediately or it may be delayed by the manner in which the ball's friction takes effect as it rolls along the ground. Now a fast straight ball and fast curve ball have been explained. Of course one could use a slow straight ball or a slow curve ball.

No kicker of note expects any of these slow deliveries or fast straight balls. Actually, what most kickers experience is trying to kick a bouncing ball, a fast moving straight bouncing ball or a fast moving bouncing curve ball. A slow bouncing straight ball is preferable to a fast smooth straight ball, and so, too, the slow bouncing curve ball to a fast moving curve ball. However, the rule states that the ball cannot bounce higher than the kicker's knee. Yeah! Try to find a consensus on that call. Remember, there are no umps. High bouncers tend to get pretty high, and kicking out from the hip is possible. I've done it! Most kickball players, real kickball players, have to learn to do it. They have to; otherwise, they're trying to get a base on balls (b.o.b.). A high base on balls percentage or number is not a good statistic to compile if one is a kicker.

One statistic everyone knew was that in 1914, the first ship transited the Panama Canal. Many unique engineering features were utilized in the concept of transiting ships from the Atlantic Ocean to the Pacific Ocean and back. The creation of a man-made lake (Gatun Lake) and a series of locks to take the ships from sea level to the lake level were constructed. The names of those locks are Miraflores Locks, Pedro Miguel Locks and Gatun Locks. To this day they are considered to be engineering feats, making the Panama Canal a Modern Wonder of the World.

In the middle of the man-made Gatun Lake is the mountaintop called Barro Colorado. It is an island that became an animal sanctuary, because the animals retreated to it, during the rising waters of the then newly created Gatun Lake. Water from the Chagras River filled Gatun Lake, which provided for the release of water into the locks to make the transit of the Isthmus possible. Perhaps the most enduring feature of the transit was the locomotion of the "mules," used in towing the ship from one lock chamber to another lock chamber. These previously diesel powered mules became electrically driven. These vehicles were ugly in a most beautiful way. Every ship making the transit was boarded by a Canal Pilot, who was responsible for guiding the ship through the entire length of the Canal.

Back to writing about pitchers and their delivery of the kickball. The pitcher can feint a pitch. That means go all the way through the windup and downswing, but not release the ball. It is not a balk! The non-delivery is a very deceptive tactic, which allows the pitcher to spin toward any hapless runners, who may have left the base, and throw the ball at them.

Pitchers learn about the kicker's weakness, because everyone knows or tells one another. Even if he is my best friend who told me his weakness, I'll tell it to the pitcher. Actually, I'll shout out from wherever I am in the field, "He doesn't like fast curve balls," but he knew I would tell, so he told me what he wanted to be pitched.

If I don't explain the other positions in the field and their purposes, it's because the pitcher is expected to "catch" all the ground balls, catch the relay throws from the field, and put out or throw out the runners. This is an immense responsibility, everyone would say so, right? And it's true! Every one of us in the field looked up to the pitcher, not just because he was probably older; which he was. And not just because he was bigger; which he was. But, because we knew that this was a "smart," "savvy," and "talented" player, who could best put the other side out. He was the "**big kid**," and I will refer to them later. The other side had to be put out for our side to become kickers in the game. (Now, workups is different, and will be explained soon.)

Putting another team out, called **side out**, meant getting three kickers or base runners out. In this regard, baseball is like kickball, saying three batters or **base runners** out. See! Once safely on first base, a player's status becomes one of being a base runner in either kickball or baseball. So, being a pitcher meant an awesome responsibility of pitching extraordinary deliveries, catching the balls being kicked (even at one's face) and putting out the base runners. The other talent of a pitcher was to tell everyone where to play in the outfield and their turn to kick. Now, one's turn at kicking was important.

The best player (kicker) was first up, and that is the **big kid**. So, the worst player would be the last kicker in the lineup. Sometimes a big kid might let his friend be the first to kick, especially if it was his birthday. That was not only a special tribute and honor, but it was a sign of good judgment. Another special tribute might happen to a "special" kid who might not play well, but would be chosen first and kick first. Everyone understood this. All of us were healthy children. Looking back upon those times makes me aware how fortunate we were. Years later, polio raised its ugly head. Many died in the United States, and there were many deaths in the Canal Zone. Many others were paralyzed, stricken or otherwise handicapped in the Canal Zone. The children growing up with them gave them special consideration.

The major concern for our parents was malaria. It was in the Canal Zone that malaria was discovered to be a mosquito borne disease. This discovery by General George Goethals started a program that continued relentlessly by spraying standing pools of water and using a fogger spray truck with DDT, which routed every street in the Canal Zone. Any instance where a rare case of malaria turned up, the individual's activities for the prior two weeks were re-visited with anti-malarial activities to eliminate the source.

So, let's go back to my earlier paragraph. Everyone now knows about the neighborhood and kickball. Oh, the kicking team just tries to score a lot more runs than the fielding team, which is why the pitcher is so important. Now one can say they know about kickball. Does anyone know what I meant by taking a break for lunch and dinner? One has to assume this is the summer because one doesn't break for lunch, if one is in school all day. If it is not summer time, all one does is break for dinner. If one were lucky, there is no homework and one can go back outside. Sometimes there is homework and no one can go back outside after dinner, "Not until the homework is finished." Ha! Many a time I "snuck" out and played kickball, until it was too dark to see before sneaking back inside our 4-family apartment. Each apartment has a front and rear door, both visible from two strategically placed chairs in the living room. These were my Mom and Dad's chairs. All 4-families were designed like this to keep kids from sneaking outside, but like all clever children it could be done! Just ask anyone that graduated from **Diablo Heights Elementary School** if they could sneak out of their 4-family apartment and not get caught. If there isn't confirmation, just ask the kids living on Davis

Street at that time, oh, late forties or early fifties. They told me they "snuck" out and that's what I told them, too.

The housing was really quite unique. The types of housing were constructed with exposed studs, being sheathed only on the exterior side. These quarters were generally without glass windows, as the windows were mainly screened. The housing or quarters were identified by the numbers of family apartments per structure, such as single family, two family, four family, twelve family and bachelor quarters. Of course, the terms cottages and duplexes were used to identify one and two family quarters. A unique feature of all the communities was that every family living in an apartment had their name on the front door of their quarters.

Now, regarding that earlier paragraph I mentioned "eating." Do I have to explain that too? Everyone knows what I mean, right? First one goes in and says they are not hungry and that they're going back outside to play. That may work. But not likely as parents have been calling one to come to dinner for a good half hour, or more, knowing that no one would until one's team got put out, or if it was workups, until one had his "ups" and got put out. But everyone could go back out and play if allowed. Usually though, before eating, one had to go clean up, remember, looking in the mirror. If one could fidget around with the water turned on full, create splashy noises, one could go to the table. Usually, one would be told to show his hands, and fidgeting around doesn't wash them, so back to the bathroom sink. Turn the water on and stick the hands under the water. "Ugh!" Then quickly dry the hands on a towel. In those days, my family didn't have all the beautiful colors, so white towels got dirty fast. Just as the waters of the Chagras River created Gatun Lake, the Chagras was also the source of public drinking water for all of the Canal Zone and Panama City. It has been said many times that if you drink of the water of the Chagras, you will return again to drink it. Walking out to the table, hands above one's head for inspection and the reward was a "harrumph," and "sit!" Let the eating begin. Remember what one hated to eat was what was being served? It was being served every night! No wonder children said they weren't hungry. Who can digest peas? Or beans? Or any other green colored vegetable? Yuk! All of this was taking time away from kickball. So, one tried secretly to feed the big dog the food. Every family had a big dog, if they had children that played kickball. Those kids grew up and I bet are feeding their big dog from the table. How else can a dog get big and come to love kickball if there wasn't this symbiosis?

Let me explain about repairing a deflated kickball. In a sense kickball provides a technical skill that could be used throughout one's life. First, one learned to fix a flat kickball. Then one learned to fix a flat bicycle tire. Finally one learned to fix an automobile's flat tire. Which of these tasks would be the most difficult? If one said repairing a kickball; that's right! So, when the smell was funny, I knew I had a leak. The kickball is inflated, right? Air can be lost in many ways, but most often a leak is caused by a puncture, a leaking stem, a canine tooth, or from sitting on it too long. The kickballs I played with were leather or canvas with a rubber inner "Bladder." There were seams holding the kickball together, and laces to keep the bladder inside. These laces had to be unlaced then re-laced closed. All the kids playing kickball could lace and unlace, tie and untie one's Keds!

One could locate the "hole" by listening to where the air came out, or where the "bladder" smell was strongest, but most of the time one would put the ball underwater to locate bubbles of escaping air. Once located, the hole could have cement glue applied on it. Immediately apply a cloth or rubber patch, holding it down firmly. It takes awhile for the glue to harden, so not playing with it until the next day is a good idea. A well made kickball will have a well-worn leather cover and a very highly patched bladder. Of course, repairing a kickball was fun! Fixing an automobile flat tire was a chore, but one could fix flat tires for a living.

Ok! I am able to and will explain workups, which is different than teams. I am implying kickball here, even though workups is applied to baseball, too. A game of workups consists of as many players as one may wish to have prior to playing teams. In other wards, one will choose up teams at some point, but until then everyone played kickball in a manner known as workups.

Whoever comes up with the idea to play kickball cries, "First ups!" It may be the one who has a good kickball and runs out onto the playing space crying, "First ups! Who else wants to play?" This is followed by shouts of "second," "third," "fourth," etc., although there is much confusion over who said second, first. This leads to chaos all the way down the line so whoever was "first up" identifies who was next to say, "second," first. Then the one who didn't call second first becomes third first. Well, get the picture? I hope! It's really not too bad as long as one calls first, first.

Speaking of firsts, the real firsts are always the pioneers and they existed in Panama, too. The pioneer families in the Canal Zone had been on the Isthmus for the construction of the Panama Railroad, which was around the middle of the 19th century. The individuals from the families of the pioneers became associated with the French Canal Commission and later with the Panama Canal Commission. Having access to one of these people was an opportunity to hear of all the scary experiences these old timers had or created for their audiences of children. OK, let's begin Chapter #2.

CHAPTER 2 - WORKUPS
This is the second of five chapters.

The sport of kickball is a sport because it involves all of the right body parts to keep an individual in good health, fitness and mentally alert. During all those years, about six, until I was twelve, I never saw an overweight kickball player. Stocky, maybe, but not chubby or fat. You see, all kickball players have to run. They run after the ball in the field, and they run the bases after they kick the ball. One can't pretend not to run "full throttle."

The kickball is a uniquely sized ball. If one is all by himself, one could shoot baskets with it. If there are two, one could play basketball one on one, or kickball with one as the kicker, while the other pitched and chased down the balls, which didn't work too well. If there are three, then one can play **dodge ball**. Remember the comment about the pitcher "throwing out the runner?" A base runner is vulnerable to being hit by the ball anytime he's off base.

So, dodge ball serves two great functions. If one were "**out**," as the thrower, it hones throwing skills at a moving target. If one were "**in**," as the dodger, it can hone one's skills at ducking, jumping, leaping and moving fast to avoid getting hit by the ball.

Those skills were especially important to escape from the jungle denizens. You didn't see the jungle, it crept out every day toward you. Things could bite you and make you really sick or dead. None of us wanted to come face to face with an angry bushmaster, coral snake or adder. For that matter the malarial mosquito and sleeping sickness fly were no better company to keep. Fire ants, bees, ticks, scorpions, spiders and our imaginations kept us on our toes, jumping at the first sight of these "guys."

Daniel G. Winklosky

Having four people gives all kinds of choices. One can still play basketball, two on two; or dodge ball, two in and two out, or one can start to play workups. (This choice is made because Al said Donna would be coming, and Johnny said Mary and Harold were on their way to play.) With four or five players one has a pitcher, kicker, infielder and the fourth or fifth player becomes the outfielder(s). Suppose one kicks the ball and gets safely to first base. Good! One can go back to the plate and kick again, the rule being that the fielders must get the runner out. Note here that there are pretend runners on the bases, which are called ghosts. This means the ghost runners score ahead of the kicker, and they count as runs.

Now, as the only kicker, if one doesn't like the pitch or delivery, one must catch the ball and throw it back to the pitcher. At that time one will tell the pitcher where one wants the ball thrown and how. There is great civility in kickball. Can anyone do that in any other sport? I think not. One may wish, but it won't happen. I've tried to do it from little league to college, maybe Herbie and Eddie tried it in the minor and major leagues. I'll have to ask them how that request went over, which means what kind of response did they get to that request.

It's a jungle out there, a dog eat dog type of world, but our jungle helped prepare us for it. Being close to the jungle was a real part of life in the Canal Zone. It was not necessary to go very far to be "in the jungle." Because of the proximity to a wild and untamed world, many Zonians found they were attracted to the jungle and its denizens, flora and fauna. Associating with headhunters of the Darien was part of the life style of several brave hearts.

Now, in workups of course one doesn't want to get put out if one is the kicker, because it means, having to be last in the outfield. If one should kick a **line drive** to the pitcher and he catches it, the kicker will exchange places with the pitcher. One

The Optimum Soul Environment

always exchanges places with the fielder who catches the fly ball. Suppose, as the base runner, one got thrown out, tagged out or hit by the ball, then one would go into the outfield and follow the "last" fielder. The rotation goes right field to center to left field, to shortstop, then to third, second and first base, pitcher then catcher. So, as a fielder, if one catches a fly ball one goes to the plate as a kicker. Now, it gets a little tricky, because if there is more than one kicker in workups and I caught a fly ball, I follow the "last" kicker in the line up.

Big dogs play this game too, but no "rules" give them status as kickers. Actually, big dogs can choose to be base runners and fielders in the same play. Big dogs can do that. Big dogs put a lot of saliva on the kickball. That factor alone makes accuracy difficult in throwing the "saliva-upped" ball. One doesn't want the big dog's saliva on the kickball if one is a fielder. I've known kickball players who could spit on the ball and hit the runner with the spit side of the ball, Yuk! (Later, those kickball players became baseball players and did this and called it a spitball. Who would believe that it was a big dog that really created that **pitch**? Here is the only homage given for this fact.) If one has a big dog, but it's a puppy, there is a point of etiquette not to bring puppies, because puppies chew up kickballs. Puppies chew up kickballs every chance they can. If one is at home and the kickball is on the bed and one owns a big dog puppy, it will get on the bed and start to chew the ball up. This means that the puppy puts a hole in it first making it go flat. Then the puppy can really sink his teeth into it, thus truly chewing it up.

Big dogs were important as companions walking in the jungle or saw grass. Where there was no jungle, the area would be overgrown with "saw grass." It was called this because the blades of grass were hard and had saw-toothed edges that literally cut you up while walking through it. Obviously, too, the blood attracted a lot of other unwanted visitors to the cuts. It was impossible, even while wearing long sleeved shirts and long pants, not to get cut walking 25 yards through such grass.

Daniel G. Winklosky

The clothes would be shredded. The tall saw grass had to be burned off every year by the Fire Department, because it became a fire hazard and a source of unwanted denizens and poisonous snakes. The young men of Balboa were often instigators of the fire on Sosa Hill, which didn't deprive the Fire Department of their job.

This is about playing **workups**. I've been trying to explain this since my first paragraph. There is no limit to the number of players that can play workups. The first four are kickers, and everyone else goes to the field. This doesn't mean one can't have more than four kickers. It would be best if there were more than four kickers. If one only has four kickers, the situation may arise where the bases are full and the kicker is out on a fly ball. The "rules" require that the fielder catching the fly ball goes to first base as a runner, and all the other base runners advance a base so that the runner on third can become the rightful kicker. Believe me, it's not easy trying to explain kickball. It helps a lot if the reader has a good imagination, and can visualize these activities taking place. Of course, one would understand better, if one ever played kickball before, or been to the Canal Zone.

For in the Canal Zone one was treated to all kinds of smells that permeated the nights and days in the tropics. Some of the most alluring aromas were from the gardenias, elang-elang, and lilies. There were other times when the air had a special smell. After a thunderstorm, the ground smelled, the pavement smelled and the ozone had a fresh clean quality about it.

There is a risk to playing workups, if one arrives late, that is. When other players have been playing a long time, they tend to quit after making an out. As I indicated earlier, a good excuse to quit after making an out is to go home to dinner. After playing kickball for six years, or more, I've heard all the excuses that have ever existed. Of course, these excuses are great prior to matriculating to junior and senior high school. Not only for high school but also for college and even later, if one became a teacher. One thing about excuses, they never change; just the verbs and nouns vary.

If one quits after making an "out," I would advise an announcement prior to one's departure, saying before one's "ups," that this is the last "round." Announcing one's intentions before "getting up," would be a wise strategy, especially if some really big kid came late to play. Big kids can intimidate smaller kids into playing longer, but not if they've heard an earlier statement that one were going home to dinner after ones last ups. I can't guarantee this ploy will work with all big kids. Some big kids, like Ray, won't let anyone quit until they've had their ups, which means everyone will have to have had their ups before he gets his turn to kick.

The heat and humidity are indescribable. To move from the shade to the sunlight was a discomfort. To walk more than a few yards was to cause one to perspire, a matter of concern to all of us. So after playing kickball for hours, our clothes were dripping with perspiration.

Anyway, big kids are important to the "rules" and workups. Remember there is no umpire, so the biggest kid becomes the dispenser of "rule-book" knowledge and sees to it that everyone plays fair. By that I mean I am not going to go and hit someone or throw the ball hard at someone smaller for catching my fly ball, or saying something about me or something I thought was "nasty." A big kid will surely mete out justice. A punch to the upper arm causes an immediate "**charley horse**." Should anyone have done really bad one might get punched on both arms. If one can't use the arms, one can't throw the ball, making one useless until the numbness subsides and the bruising pain can be tolerated. As I said before, civility is a part of kickball, which one can learn, whenever one is ready, because this is the beginning of good sportsmanship.

Before leaving these precepts on philosophy and value systems, lets just say a few words about being sociable. No one can play kickball alone! That's a fact! If one has a kickball, one must learn to share it with others and watch it get terribly abused at times, even go soft for lack of air. Like so many other facets of kickball, playing and sharing one's kickball is a major evolution in a child's life. Once one has gone beyond sharing their kickball and leaving it so others can continue playing, then **brotherhood and genuine friendship** are the next lessons one comes to learn and appreciate. Wouldn't you really like to be playing in a game of workups right now? Honestly?

Building character and other qualities are philosophies one learns to adopt playing kickball, as a young kid. When one is 5 or 6 or 7, even 8, one is or was a young kid. A big kid is twelve years old or older. Some eleven-year-olds looked big, too. My purpose in defining these terms will be more evident later, as I begin to use them.

"What you see is what you get" in the tropics meant seeing a plethora of trees, plants, and grasses. They were a panorama of every imaginable hue of green and yellow. The brilliance of the blue of the sky and the white of the clouds produce a vision of delightful amazement. Added to all these colors were the myriad of colors from flowers and fruits. These were the reds, blues, purples, oranges, browns and yellows. It was not a seasonal experience, but because of the uniqueness of the tropics, these were the colors seen year round.

While I am on the subject of character building, one won't find any poor loser playing kickball for the following reasons. Everyone wants to be the pitcher or kicker. Everyone can't have his way all at once, so patience is built into the conduct of play. Unlike baseball where pitches can really get errant, kickball deliveries are mostly close to the plate, close enough to go and kick the ball. OK? Because of this truism, one doesn't have fielders "whining," in kickball or saying, "Let him hit the ball! Throw it over the plate! Can't you pitch? Can't you hit?" These are never voiced phrases, because good sportsmanship follows from friendship.

There are no coaches or parents at kickball workups. I recall that that's good. If a parent showed up at workups, it was probably bad. It was bad news for their child. They are probably real late for dinner! They may even get spanked. But kickball does engender a sense of fearlessness, and our chum walks bravely off the field to his most certain doom. Not all parents act that way, but most have not kept the quality of patience for being late very high on their character retention list. By the age of 30 most adults have "lost" the great lessons taught by kickball, and so it is difficult to trust anyone over 30 or anyone without kickball's virtues.

Every fisherman remembers the corbinas, barracudas, snappers, groupers, and blowfish and, yes sharks, lots of sharks in the waters of the canal and oceans. Fishing along the causeway was as important as school to the youth in the Canal Zone, as much as it was perhaps to Huckleberry Finn on the Mississippi River in the States. Summers were a time out of school, but more importantly, a time to fish both during the day and night. In the meantime one discovered the marine life of Panama, but buzzards, iguanas, and golden frogs are part of the many colorful denizens that inhabit the tropics.

Just as big kids provide the roles of umpires, they also serve the sport as coaches. Would anyone want someone playing who couldn't throw or run? Of course not! Someone must teach the smaller kids. That is what the older kids and big kids do. Remember the "charley horse?" Big kids explain themselves just once. No **deficit attention span** is another remarkable quality about kickball. If one thought they would like to count the blades of grass that are trampled or see the animals in the clouds overhead, while being in the outfield, a big kid could give a "**heads up**," right then and there. A "heads up" is like a "charley horse," but hurts more, because it's the side of the ear that feels numb. Of course, if one were really "out there in space," a "heads up" and a couple of "charley horses" register **reality** immediately and stay until its time for one's ups.

Coaching is not all that bad in sports today, but *only in kickball can you induce a sense of reality and attention focusing*, without going to jail for a crime. All young kids knew they would become the big kids. These were valuable lessons on how to teach. Again, only in kickball can one learn to appreciate that one becomes a big kid soon, and has a lot of responsibilities, when that time comes.

The statements attributed to Vince Lombardi, that "Champions are made not born," must have been a recollection from his days at kickball tournaments. It is at tournaments that champions are crowned as champions. Winners are made champions, see? But in kickball everyone is on the team, playing, winning and then being crowned a champion.

Other figures of speech like "An' now by the grace of God, it's my turn!" This referred to one's time to kick. Of course, an adult older than 30 might say, "there but for the grace of God, go I" turned around this thought. I would add, "and probably to the outfield!" Kickball players are proud to be who they are and who their teammates are. So everyone played kickball in the neighborhood. It was an inevitability of growing up on Davis Street in the 1940's.

When the number of players exceeded fourteen, it was then an almost sure thing that an older, bigger kid would say, "Let's divvy up and play teams." If there was only one big kid, he made up the teams. Otherwise, there would be two big kids and they would choose sides, alternating in picking their players. This was to be the greatest lesson for all kickball players, learning to await being picked and being grateful for it! It wasn't like the big kid didn't know everyone. Each kid has been around since being three years old and now one is almost eight. That's five years and that's a long time.

The Optimum Soul Environment

Playing team kickball was serious stuff, but I've been preparing for it. Team play is what champions are made of "not Wheaties," another over the age of 30 compromises. Team play is what I am writing about in Chapter #3. Does one need an invitation to turn the page? Turn the page or one may expect a "heads up" or "charley horse."

Daniel G. Winklosky

CHAPTER 3 - TEAMS
This is the third of five chapters.

A lot of books have extolled the values learned in team play and the sacrifices made by individuals for the good of the team. That's all well and good. But remember, those authors are all over 30 years old. One can't expect a pure exposition by them on these subjects. Ask any ten-year old kickball team player about values and sacrifice and their answer will be, "Huh? What's that mean – value, sacrifice?"

It's confusing to the ten-year old. (I used that age because a younger kid would know even less about team play.) Before becoming twelve years old and a big kid, all a young kid's knowledge about team play was shaped by the big kid or captain of the team (one and the same thing). The big kid was pitcher and kicked first. That's it! Around that example everyone else became acknowledged for their skills in the field or as a kicker and was placed in the field and line up, accordingly. One always followed the kicker that was a little better or a lot better than one was. How can that be a value? How is that a sacrifice? Team play was about playing as best you could, now that is a value. Where one played was never discussed or debated, because if one didn't know one's skill level the big kid did and put everyone in the field and in the kicking lineup where he saw fit. I have not used he/she or him/her types of descriptions, because any girl that was the big kid, playing kickball, was a "Tomboy."

Girls played kickball and played it exceptionally well. But they weren't called girls, just kids, because everyone was a kid. Any female, playing kickball, who was over 11 or 12, was not only a tomboy, but also a big kid! The tomboy moniker could only have been coined in kickball, because girl kids could dodge, throw and run. These are the talents acknowledged by all kickball players. I followed girl kid kickers often in my career.

For some reason, tomboys stopped playing by the time they were between eleven and twelve. It is also true that boys at age thirteen stopped playing kickball. The transition of our youths, moving away from kickball, is an **unexplainable phenomenon**. Historians and even the natural selection theories of Darwin were written after they were 30 years old, but this phenomenon had nothing to do with natural history or natural selection. But, maybe it had something to do with the "boy loves girl thing" or something like that. Boys and girls are never the same again! They are different. Kickball was never played on grounds of boy/girl differences. All neighborhoods need everyone to be able to get up a game of teams. Young kids. All kids. This also worked well for neighborhood celebrations.

Community celebrations brought us all together to play kickball. The celebration of the Fourth of July in the Canal Zone was no different than "Anywhere," USA. The fireworks display was conducted on Sosa Hill, a geographic feature that could be seen from most every community around Balboa. Perhaps not as elegant as today's versions of displays, the drama was always exceeding our modest expectations. The fireworks were truly a bridge between the Zonian and the events taking place on "Main Street," USA.

Team play had nothing to do with sacrifice. I mean giving up dinner so I could play kickball; how much of a sacrifice is that? The sport of kickball is not altogether a democratic institution. If one can have an umpire, captain and rule maker all in one big kid, that can't be a democracy. But it was a sport with rules none the less, and big kids saw fit to honor those rules. What I'm trying to say is this paper is not about politics, see? But kickball is not a dictatorship! **The sport of kickball is more like a republic**. Everyone was encouraged to become greater than he was the day before. That was the role of the older kids. They saw to everyone's personal and authentic improvement. A majority of younger kids would just not say that they didn't want to play with that big kid. Kickball was my life. How can I explain it any better, and to be playing team kickball was what life was all about. To be on a kickball team was what Shakespeare meant by "To be or not to be!" (Prove to me he didn't mean that!)

I don't know what "being a team player" really means, especially when one looks at today's professional teams. Kickball, as a team sport, is one in which the big kid makes all the other kids better than all the other teams' kids. From this premise tournament victories are attained, and when one wins the big one everyone on the team becomes a champion. There weren't trophies in those days. Probably one got a medal, or else a ribbon, or most likely a certificate, which is a piece of printed paper, denoting one as a champion. OK. Think about champions for a moment. The pitcher and first kicker, our big kid, beat the other team's big kid; we younger kids were along for the ride. Our roles were to chase down the balls in the field or run the bases until we got put out. That's team play! Sacrifice? Except for skipping dinners, I don't know about any such concepts, or feelings or big kid's words to do this or that as a sacrifice for the good of the team. The big kid was the team. He was the coach. He said and did what he felt was necessary to win the kickball game. At eight years old, how could I be expected to know about sacrifice? Maybe the poorer performing baseball teams in the major leagues should spend the off seasons playing kickball. Maybe, just maybe, they might discover how champions are made, and discover a "big kid" in the process to tell them where to play in the field and when to bat next!

Enough about all that; I want to reveal the pleasure of playing team kickball. Well, one more digression, OK? There was a "recess" in elementary school. This meant that Miss Brown's 3rd grade class was going to play as a team against our Mrs. Brooks' 3rd grade class. That meant all 26 kids of Mrs. Brooks' class were in the field, and all 23 kids in Miss Brown's class were to have first ups. No one was prepared for making a kicking lineup or fielding assignments; such chaos! Young

The Optimum Soul Environment

kickball players really are dependent upon the organizational skills of a big kid. A half hour recess meant that sometimes Mrs. Brooks' team would have been in the field the whole time. But everyone still had fun, playing kickball. In adult terms our play may have been close to being appallingly "slipshod." If Mrs. Brooks asked our class if we wanted to play Mrs. Wright's 4th grade class in kickball next recess, all 26 of us would shout, "Yes!" Teachers didn't arrange for kickball at every recess, probably just once a week. Other recesses were for dodge ball, hopscotch, running and of course workups. All these were great recess activities, because it was honing everyone to be better at kickball, all of us. In dodge ball at recess, watch out for Julia who throws a "wicked" curve ball.

No one but an adult over 30 says, "time is running out!" Even if we didn't get our ups, during recess, we were playing kickball. Time never runs out. Recesses came and went. The school year came and went, a lot of them! The summers came and went. But time never ran out then, or even now, as I write these remembrances. Since I'm now twice older than 30, I'm trust worthy. Not because adults say my "Time is running out," but because the second childhood is a "real phenomenon." What would you really like to be doing? I would like to be playing kickball! Wouldn't you?

A lot of books have been written on geriatrics, and about the "baby boomer" generation. The "baby boom" was a mild population explosion in the Canal Zone, following **WWII**. Most of us were 9 or 10 and had a baby brother or sister. In my case my brother and I had a baby sister, Mary Ann. We couldn't wait for her to grow up and play kickball with us and take her to the States to show her off to our cousins.

Vacation time accrued very quickly for those employed overseas. If one agreed to work two more years, an employee could receive a free trip to the USA, which was usually taken every two years for periods of a month or more. These trips were very important to the Zonian. These vacations allowed the

Zonian families to spend time with their hometown friends and families.

Hmmmm! I digressed more than I thought possible. In team kickball there were two types of team games. One team game was just neighborhood kids at play. The other team game was representing "Diablo Heights." The town games were played in the gymnasium to a packed "house," filling the bleacher section along one wall of the gymnasium. All the other neighborhood children attended. If one were too young to go alone, or with a baby sitter, one's parent (Mom or Dad) would go. It was free! It didn't cost your parents anything to go, but usually only one went along. Go figure! If nothing else could set the heart on fire, these games would!

The Diablo Heights team held practices, too. One could go and sit in the bleachers at the gym and watch these workouts, usually with a Royal Crown Cola in one's hands. This is not an endorsement; it was the biggest bottle with the most fluid for the least cost. Even as an aside, kickball was valuable for imparting lessons in economics. (I don't understand economics today. They keep putting less fluid in bottles and charging a lot more. A postage stamp was three cents back then, but is now over 30 cents.) I have just enumerated how kickball taught economics to the youth of Diablo Heights, and presumably elsewhere in the Canal Zone.

"Buy low sell high" would not have any meaning to a kickball player. But fake a low throw and throw high, or visa versa, would be meaningful. Someone named Adam Smith established the laws of economics, Mr. Laffer gave his name to an important economic curve, Mr. Gresham proposed that bad money drove out good money, and another adult stated that scarcity caused an imbalance in supply and therefore demand. These words always get twisted around by those over thirty. The saying in kickball was "supply on demand," which meant throw me the ball, or give it to me, now. The dollar bill stated pay the bearer on demand one silver dollar, not a pile of silver

The Optimum Soul Environment

dust! (You can't now, because it isn't the same dollar bill anymore; remember the postage stamps aren't the same now, either.) It meant that you could trust the dollar bill to hold its value, just as one would trust the big kid to hold one's change to keep from dropping it or losing it during a kickball game. Silver certificates could be exchanged for a silver dollar anytime one wanted. All the kickball players knew that, but one silver dollar is all that was needed for the hope chest. I had one silver dollar my whole childhood. (Maybe the economic demise is linked to the fact one can't get a silver dollar in exchange for today's dollar.) Maybe all the distrust and rule changes one experiences after age thirty made for recessions, or boom and bust economies. I'm not saying farmer's crops fail, or governments collapse or corporations fold because kickball's virtues are lost. But who's to say? But still, if one is out of a job, in debt or bankrupt, I'd say the best thing to do right then, right now, is play kickball.

To the kid playing kickball, life's lessons came one at a time, but never at a time one couldn't handle them. Life was just not complicated as a kid. Isn't that true too today for adults? Now I really have been digressing – sorry!

Team play consisted of nine players per side in tournaments. Any number of players could be up or in the field in neighborhood play. When the Diablo Heights team practiced, other neighborhood kids were asked to play against them. Usually all the big kids in the neighborhoods were on the Diablo Heights team. So, when a neighborhood big kid said come to the gym and practice against the "Diablo Heights" team, this was an honor, believe me. I became a big kid. After I became a big kid, the tournament teams had ceased, and a league was formed into A, B, C, D and E team age groups.

The learning curve to become a big kid was very gradual, which taught some sense of humility and trust especially in the Creator, or whatever one's religion, because everyone played together. There was no cursing or swearing. Kickball was played, but it was like dancing, as our bodies were in motion to an unsung rhythm. There was no music to play to, but the shouts of the players, chasing down the ball, throwing at base runners, and the dodging of the ball by the base runners was unlike any other sport. Everyone seemed to be in a flow, a transcendental state of pleasure! Successfully dodging the thrown ball continued the flow of the game. Even when all the base runners stopped at base, the flow of excitement continued on a constant high. All were free spirits! I didn't say that, but that was how I felt then. Being a free spirit must have been the word that parents used to describe their child while outside playing kickball. From ages 6 to 12, who can identify with a religion, or any religious philosophy? A philosophy of life, though, was being imparted throughout those six years of playing in the neighborhood.

In kickball one was learning about social values, economics, religion, trust, respect, and elder worship. (Big kids and movie stars were our heroes, not our parents, as that would not happen until we became over thirty years old ourselves.) As stated earlier, no other sport develops such great eye-hand (throwing) and eye-foot (kicking) coordination, and one can throw in running and dodging as well. Kickball brought holistic action into our conscious and unconscious moments. Soundness of body, mind, heart and spirit was the reward for enjoying kickball all those years.

I suppose some kickball-playing kids may have stopped playing, during that six year span. There could have been a lot of reasons for that to happen. Some parents moved to a foreign country where the children didn't play kickball. Some kids had "soft" bones and had to stop because they were always breaking an arm or leg, or some were military "brats," or preacher's kids (PK), or a child of a corporate representative that moved to somewhere else every two years. A lot of us learned to value the here and now, because tomorrow one might not be able to play kickball with one's buddies anymore. The movement of others away from the neighborhood or Canal

The Optimum Soul Environment

Zone was not all bad. It developed telephone buddies or pen pals. Writing was not a highly developed skill among kickball players, and I must admit my letters were written less and less frequently. Once a year perhaps became never again, but the friendship always remained. It would be something incredible to see all those kids again, because they were part of "your big family."

The extended family so typical in the United States, did not exist for the military and civilian personnel, except in a few cases. Because of this, everyone helped one another in a closeness every bit as important as that of the typical extended family of the States.

Team play began with the choosing of sides, unless another neighborhood of kids came to play us. This was OK. Playing other neighborhood kids meant everyone learned geography. One learned all about one's own town, in my case "Diablo Heights." I can still draw a pretty good street map of Diablo. Street name maps for all of the communities were found in the pages of the telephone directory. I remember that at one time a large community plan was erected at the entrance to Diablo Heights. As indicated before the names of every family was on the door of each of the housing quarters.

Anyway, all kids, no matter what part of town they lived in, could join in a game of kickball, wherever that game was being played. This unrestricted acceptance inherent in kickball should suggest to our world leaders to take up this sport. Go to the next page, which is Chapter #4.

Daniel G. Winklosky

CHAPTER 4 - PICK ME! PICK ME!

The greatest story ever told, the greatest lesson ever learned and the greatest chapter ever written is the same title as the title of this book. This is a true story, lesson and chapter.

In a society that allows freedom to choose that which is the best for the occasion, kickball reaches its highest moral accomplishment. Neighborhood games, Diablo Heights neighborhood intra-rivalry games and the Diablo Heights league games were played as team games. From the moment a kid plays his first team game until his last kickball game he is given the greatest opportunity to accept life on its real terms, but without crushing hopes and expectations.

Playing kickball and living in the Canal Zone involved travelling, which was always an experience. The Panamanian bus of special note for its wild experiences was the Chiva. A colorfully painted exterior with a unique name gave it it's identity. The Chiva driver spent most of his time blowing the horn and pushing down on the accelerator. Within the interior of the bus, the seats ran parallel down the sides, so that passengers are looking at those seated across from them and the aisle was filled with packages and bags, forming a hurdle of major proportions. Stopping the bus was a special talent. One may just say "parada" (which means halt and voiced in one's best Spanish dialect). Failing to get the bus to stop usually brought out the unique phrase, "for God's sake parada!"

Every game generally involved choosing up sides by the biggest kids. Although scoring more runs than the other team was the desired goal, playing a good game of kickball was the main purpose. With that in his mind the big kid chose his team very carefully. That is until the end of the line. It probably didn't matter to the outcome of the game how an 8–year old kid would play or that he was kicking last. But it did to me. I never wanted to kick last, or play right field, but I did. A lot! When I made the "Diablo Heights" team I was kicking last and playing right field. But, I was playing for the Diablo Team! And I was older than eight.

When I was 8-years old, I liked to stand in the front when big kids chose up sides. "Pick me! Pick me," I was saying in my conscious thoughts and by standing there. Sometimes I would see another 8-year old come right out and say, "Pick me! Pick me!" Alas. It was the worst thing anyone could do or say! Big kids truly would purposely ignore him until the very last player to be chosen. If the choosing up came down to an odd-man out it was up to the big kids to make the decision, "does he play?" Usually, the last player chosen and the odd-man out rotated playing, alternating innings. Otherwise it was "one potato, two potato, three" or "eenie, meenie, miney, moe," and "you're out!" That meant one couldn't play until someone would have to go home for dinner or someone else came to play. That was surely one's fate should one utter "Pick me, Pick me." I only did it once. From then on I stood in front of the players and thought "Pick me, Pick me." Guess what? The big kids knew that. It always surprised me when a big kid pointed his finger at me and said, "I pick you."

I pick you. Aren't those the greatest sounds and words in the whole wide world? *I pick you.* By the time one is a lot older one is also a better player, and the big kid would just say, "I pick Danny." The first time I heard my name was wow he knows me. (Of course, he lives two houses down Davis Street, and has been your baby-sitter for years, though not as often now. I couldn't put those mature reflections together back then.) So, wow, the big kid has chosen me (not last) and knows my name. I had a lot of experience standing there thinking "Pick me, Pick me," even when I was chosen to kick second and play infield, by either big kid. Eventually, I would become a big kid and have to do the choosing.

I tried hard. It was my intention to really play well for the big kid. Not so we might win as much as to make the big kid aware I hustled after the ball and ran around the bases as fast as I could, or faster than it looked like I could. I never wanted to get picked last. I never wanted to kick last, no one did. I never wanted to get picked lower than I thought I should have been. Here again, if pride showed outwardly, one would be ignored on purpose. One learned about these things by perceptive reflection when going to bed at night or was told by an older kid what was what. That was worth listening to, and older kids, not the big kid, helped younger kids think things out, not always with subtle hints. "**Ha! Doncha know why** you didn't get picked before Tommy?" I'll say more about this later, but it made one think. If one hadn't figured it out by bedtime, then one did some reflecting on the day's actions, before falling asleep. **Coming to terms with reality didn't just occur from the choosing process.** The choosing process included how one had been playing their position, base running and kicking. I relived the whole day's events to see which of them might negatively affect being chosen the next day. Self-assessment, each night, was necessary to attain the right frame of mind as to how to play kickball better the next day, and that reflection came before my prayers.

If I decided that night that I had thrown the ball a little too hard at Connie, I made it a point the next day to apologize to her. Others had said similar things to me in my early years of kickball. An eight-year old isn't going to throw a ball too hard at a ten-year old. Besides, if the ten-year old thought differently he'd tell you right there, right then, and one might get a "charley horse." Then the big kid might give the ten-year old a "charley horse." I don't remember much of that scenario actually happening, after all, the ten-year old could throw the ball hard enough to knock one's legs out from under. I went tumbling a lot during those years when my legs went out from under me. These were neighborhood activities.

The Optimum Soul Environment

When the time came that I was picked to play for the "Diablo Heights" team all the lessons I had learned created for games of **good sportsmanship**. One had to play smart, one had to play hard (all out effort), and one had to believe in one's self and one's teammates. The concept of being on a team, and that they were my teammates was wonderful. It took a longer period of time to think of me being their teammate. But it happened. Teammates are friends for life! It didn't matter that we continued to play against each other in our neighborhoods. We were teammates on the "Diablo Heights" team. I wrote earlier, brothers and sisters are special. I loved them. Teammates didn't replace family, somehow or other teammates became like family! (Even now I cannot tell what I mean by that. It was not the same kind of family love, nor was it reverence, and it was more than to aid one another or to help one another; it was a bond of mutual trust. Yes!)

If while playing one got hurt, each of the teammates is checking on you. If Timmy was a base runner, and it looked like Timmy was going to get thrown out, I might have shouted "throw at me," knowing I could dodge the ball easily from where they were, and distract them long enough to have allowed Timmy to slide into base safely. My examples lack something unless one can recall one's own experiences of being a teammate to understand what a teammate means. Would I recognize my teammates now from back then? Probably not! Would I then have the same feelings for them now? Yes! How could that be proven? I guess Oprah would have to reunite us!

The concept of revenge would not have been a young kid's emotion, and if it had, after six years of kickball, greed, revenge, hate and depression (associated with the first three emotions) would no longer be apparent. It would take about twenty years, after age 30, for these emotions and depression to be experienced by us as adults.

Concern for one's "Diablo Heights" teammates would translate into concern for one's neighborhood and later for everyone at large. Being a good kickball player, a good sport, and a teammate put these games on a high level of good sportsmanship, physical ability and spiritual activity. The team captain was an especially important honor. Teammates selected the captain. He would have been an older kid, but there would have been many older kids equal to the honor. There were two ballots. The first to select the captain; the second a unanimous vote of endorsement by the whole team. Only in kickball!

It is hard to find a kickball in the sporting goods stores, today. We didn't have sporting goods stores in the Canal Zone, but they did in Panama City. And they sold kickballs. In the **CZ** *we had commissaries and one could buy the brand that was stocked, which our parents most often did, unless they went into Panama City to a sporting goods store to buy a special ball for one's birthday or for one's Christmas present. Fourth of July Avenue, Central Avenue, Front Street and J Street were familiar names and destinations for the Zonians shopping in Panama City. There was little that could not be found to buy. What one paid was conditioned by bartering, for no price was fixed, it was simply a matter of finding a value acceptable to both parties. Even when walking out of the store without coming to an agreed price, the air was charged with a buy/sell emotion and some turned around and went back and sometimes the salesman came out to say, "OK!" Smiles predominated these transactions, even when there was no sale, the departing customer might say "Tu queres mas que yo!" to the shop keeper, who would smile and say, "very, very good quality!"*

The kickball was a symbol of unity, not because it was round or circular! We "loaned" our kickballs out if we were sick or could not leave the house. One might not get it back for days, weeks, or months if one's family were taking a trip or vacation. It was not an occasion for alarm. It was given to others so they could play kickball in your absence. No big deal! Others were doing the same thing throughout the year.

The Optimum Soul Environment

Remember the term I used earlier, "Doncha know?" It was a rhetorical statement and always was followed by the word "why," such as **doncha know why** you were thrown out running the bases? Why you missed catching the fly ball? Why you caused the other team to score their last two runs? And so on. If by chance one didn't figure it out and repeated the mistake in the following days that kid would whap you or slap your shoulder hard and say, "Dincha figure it out?" Even a big kid would concur with that roughhouse treatment to make the point to think it out again. Today's generation says, "Go figure."

If children don't have good reasoning skills, today, one must admit that the lack of kickball in society has had its price after all. Coming up with an answer and modifying one's kickball tactics was the only way to be able to respond to the doncha know edict. One can call that linear conceptualization, inductive reasoning, creative thinking, but kickball kids wouldn't understand that. What was so very important about these paragraphs was that no one was demeaned with statements like – That was stupid! Are you an idiot? What's the matter with you? (Kickball players were not subjected to the verbal harassment that you can hear today on playgrounds and in major league sport stadiums, arenas, and ice hockey rinks.)

It is important to note that kickball couldn't provide an understanding of everything. I'll explain this in more philosophical terms in a minute. I mentioned that everyone played kickball in the neighborhood, and that was true, at least for a couple of years. But there were other reasons for neighborhood friends to drop out of kickball. Some times another kid chose to practice music lessons. There were other kids who were drawn to explore the jungle, because Panama was basically a jungle. It is my belief though that the lessons in kickball during those formative years enabled these kids to excel in their ability and talent. (Today, I would not be surprised if they became accomplished symphony orchestra performers or that their jungle experiences, coupled with kickball, made them expert entomologists.)

Our school grade system in the Canal Zone was Kindergarten, Elementary 1-6; Junior High School 7-8; and High School 9-12. It was the best educational system in the world. How you would disprove that would interest me. Please know that the high school teaching system mandated that at a minimum, teachers were required to have masters' degrees. This created a very strong curriculum for all the students and parents could be confident and supportive of the educational system.

Neither the educational system nor kickball prepared me for being naked in a gang shower such as in gym class in junior high school and that was just the beginning. I tried to hide my private parts, as did everyone else. It was called sexual awareness. I'm still a little self-conscious.

In kickball, the big kid made everyone feel like princes or princesses, because someday everyone would become a big kid. So throughout elementary school one felt OK and everyone else felt Ok about themselves and others. Junior High School tended to be a drifting time that may have begun a break down of the concepts and virtues learned in kickball. *Strange how things happen. Confirmation of these thoughts appeared in my morning paper, The Korean Herald.*

Another disquieting and unsettling fact was that High School had a King and a Queen. Only a few people could be either of those, so all the rest of the students were classified as "student body," referring to the whole school, or a caste system of identities such as freshman, sophomore, junior or senior class. Of course I wanted to be a senior the first day of my freshman year. We weren't dummies yet! For three years one was in the shadows of the upper classmen, and none of them forgot your diminished status. Even the big kids I used to know had grown beyond their recognition of me. And sad to say, by the time I became a senior, my big kid qualities that I had in kickball towards the younger kids were submerged somewhere in my subconscious.

High School had organized junior and senior varsity sports. I played all the sports with the exception of swimming. I found fulfillment in track, baseball, basketball and football. It was like one had to play all of these sports to experience in a year what one could achieve in one game of kickball!

If one hadn't lost those kickball virtues by the time one completed high school one could try again to do so by going on to college. Or at least, that was what it seemed like to me, a major repetition of high school.

Somehow, when one's age is greater than 60, the childhood unconscious, suppressed values, emotions and remembrances return. It is a very rewarding state of being, and one should look forward to it in turn. I say that because there truly is something rare, like a whole new persona, embodying purity, truth and innocence all at once. Awareness of this makes old age a pleasure for me. Perhaps this is apropos of the Royal Palm Tree, which lined the Prado and many prominent open spaces in the Canal Zone. The Royal Palm Tree reaches maturity after 100 years, then it blooms, and dies. Those Royal Palm trees planted in the early 1900's are coming to maturity and will soon be blooming. Sadly, they will also be dying.

I should like to promulgate a new resurgence in kickball, for those my age and older. So, Tinker, Owen, Dorman, Julia, Augie, whoever and wherever you are, let's meet at the gym and play kickball again!

I return to the concept of sexual awareness of young people going into and through puberty. This period of time goes beyond the teen years and actually spans the period of 13 or so, to 25 or so! I did not have a clue of what this part of my life was all about. It never came up as a subject in kickball. Sure I had a girlfriend, but I had boyfriends, too. But that wasn't enough! One was just not prepared for sexual awareness, and the next twelve years were a painfully difficult adjustment. I know. I had to live through them. One could really compound difficulties, during that time. Know what I mean? To top it all off one probably got married before 24 and had kids before one was 26. Many teenagers and young adults thoroughly enjoyed this time in their lives. I just think they were the exception or in the minority. I make these statements because it means I won't have to get letters of rebuttal from Luis or Roger, etc. Like I said, there were kings and queens, the rest of us were the subjects. I wish we could have played kickball in high school, boys against the girls! This is suggested as a means or method to generate social and sexual awareness.

Having a chaperone on a date, was a long-standing custom when dating a young Panamanian lady. Although this custom was not a part of the Canal Zone dating scene, there were few places that young couples could go to, as the Zonian police patrolled every area of the Zone that could be a "lover's lane."

Anyway, by the time one is over 60, one has gained sexual awareness and becomes a patient and spontaneous partner. One becomes aware of the unique quality of intimacy in a relationship.

By now one must be wondering why I chose the title, **"Pick Me! Pick Me!"** Life is a series of choices, for me and for others. Everything I have been writing about has implied that our life reflects the times when each of us is picked, which continues even until our deaths. Some might argue that even death is an act of one's being chosen to die!

Throughout all these years and all these experiences I wanted on many occasions to say, "Pick me, Pick me!" You know what I'm talking about. Somewhere deep inside came the lessons of kickball. One prepared each night for the next day of kickball. Later, one prepared to make the varsity team. One prepared for acceptance to college. One prepared for that first job and all the other jobs.

What one couldn't prepare for was being rejected unfairly or unjustly. It didn't matter that it was just *office politics*. That didn't make sense then and doesn't really now, looking back over those occasions. There aren't those consoling words, "Doncha know why" you didn't get picked? But one thought that, and went to bed reflecting on the process and activities that had brought one to this point of questioning. There would be an answer, and one just had to really concentrate on it. Eventually one made a decision as to what the answer was. If one could make the changes one did; if not, one opted for other opportunities to be chosen.

When young kids represent purity, truth and innocence, why do adults want to change them? In retrospect, it would appear that a republic such as the USA inculcates those qualities throughout a lifetime! As a matter of fact, after one becomes 60 and a grand parent, that's the responsibility with the grandchildren, and one knows it! "Doncha?" Even though one may encourage the grandchildren to play kickball, one can't meddle with their parents' ideas of raising their children. All of us have to honor that. One also hopes that one's children's kickball values will awaken in time for them to teach their kids to play kickball. Then all the generations can play! Maybe not grandma, but let her be the one to decide, because she might be a good ump! I never had grandparents in the CZ, nor did any of us on Davis Street. I don't really know what grandparents can do with a kickball. Does anyone?

Our parents played on a rare occasion, such as celebrations and children's birthday parties. They couldn't run anymore, and were funny when they tried. I don't let that image worry me. I'll play right field, kick last and run the bases as best I can, and look as funny as I can, doing it.

Daniel G. Winklosky

Back then, there were lots of parties and celebrations, but none compared to Carnival. Throughout the Latin world, the Carnival was a yearly activity that took precedence over all other matters. True, the Mardi Gras of New Orleans and the Carnival of Rio de Jenerio were the most important locations, but everyone in Panama knew it was time to party and did. Singing, dancing, drinking and parades dominate the three days of Carnival. The Zonian was not a typical part of this experience, unless invited into the atmosphere of a family in Panama. There was very little, or a token at best, cultural interchange between Panama and the Canal Zonian families. It was unusual for a Zonian to speak Spanish, while most Panamanians found it desirable to learn English. By the middle of the 1970's, the Spanish language was a common second language on the Zone and cultural, intellectual or financial barriers had ceased.

Perhaps the greatest Greek philosopher was Plato. He wrote in his book, "The Republic," about the virtues of having young kids running, throwing, jumping, kicking, dodging, and having fun. Like so many other mysteries of the "Old World," we have to make assumptions about what game that ancient Greek was suggesting. My guess is that it was kickball! Ergo! Kickball was played in Athens, Greece, and those children grew up to be Olympian athletes. Maybe I can't aspire to be like Plato, but I do wish our young people could grow up, having fun again, like we did!

In ancient and modern India, the religious teachings suggest that individuals come into this lifetime (and many others) for a special reason. **Doncha know why?** Our generation came into this lifetime to play kickball and keep kickball's values preserved for future generations. Another way of stating this theme is "that was our fate." We are to accept that fate, which is the greatest lesson we have to learn, and then continue to play and teach kickball!

Even the greatest of Zen followers would attribute the kickball maxim, "Honor the potential of all things and all people," as being a highly beneficial way toward right living, Nirvana!

Can one imagine Dante writing about the angels. Wouldn't he depict them in an imaginary scenario with cherubs and angels in front of the Creator jumping up and down saying, **"Pick me!** *Pick me to go to earth to be born, and to grow up to play kickball!"* Is that how I came to be born? It would certainly explain a lot, if that were how we came to be born. It would make understanding the saying of Jesus, "that we are not of the earth, but in the earth" a lot easier! Well, think about it and let me know how Dante would have expressed pre-destination!

Kickball was not a religion, because folks in the Canal Zone had religion, lots of them. My father was called JEW, also my brother and his oldest son. I attended the church that combined a lot of Protestant precepts on religion. It was called the "Union Church." But I was good at catechism, too! I would help my friend, Billy, learn his lessons so we could go out and play kickball.

Most religious philosophies, ethnic cultures, entrepreneurial minds, and the adventuring spirit were a part of the history and make up of the communities in the Canal Zone. A melting pot of immigrants, an equatorial jungle, and a mission that was to make ships move from the Atlantic to the Pacific were the ingredients of our communities.

All this great social planning in the Canal Zone gave me a greater insight and appreciation for the Creator's planning skills in creating the solar system, galaxies and universes.

I know this is a long chapter, but it's because of the length of the title. You would never say, "Don't pick me," because I'm ill or I hurt too much to play. Everyone played hurt. One played even if suffering from asthma. One played as long as one could, even if it was only malaria. I wasn't the only kid with asthma. Sure one had scabs on the knees! And elbows! And scabs on top of one another. And yes one ran a little funny trying to protect those scabs from being hit by the ball, while running the bases and dodging the ball. It hurt when the ball smacked the scab!

In the gym one was sliding on the wood floor, getting floor burns! That was better than sliding on the asphalt of the street. Sliding on the dirt, gravel and grass created scabs called raspberries, which made bathing painful. Even my parents couldn't stand the screams when the water hit that part of the body, so I didn't have to bathe for a couple days. But playing hurt was heroic! All the great legends of sports and movies succeeded against great odds while hurt. Everyone identified their scabs with the heroes wounds and understood their pain and heroic accomplishments. A kickball player's imagination was infinite in its heroic depiction. Going out in search of adventure meant leaving the neighborhood. It happened around ten years of age. One went in search of more kickball games. Like Aegeas and Hercules before him and all the heroes after them, one set forth to conquer all that was bad and right all that was wrong. I "kind'a" felt that way, right?

Aegeas
An excellent kickball player, he was the folk hero of legendary Athens. Aegeas was the embodiment of the heroic Hercules. Aegeas overcame the villainous and evil ones and in the same manner that they slew their victims he slew them. Aegeas also slew the minotaur, a half-human half horse that feasted on the first born of the Athenian families, and thus Aegeas ended that cycle of death for the Athenians.

Hercules
A superior homerun kicker, Hercules was the patron of Sparta, just as Athena was the patron of Athens. The mythical adventures of Hercules were against the great

legends of those days, such as the Titans, which he subdued to allow mankind to be the stewards of the earth.

Even at Christmas time, today, I am reminded that the beat of the little drummer boy song came from a big kid in kickball saying, "and he told me kick a home run! Kick a home run!"

Christmas trees were blue spruces, shipped to the Canal Zone and the Christmas tree truck from the commissary came down every street to delivery the trees. Every family had paid in advance for their tree, and so they were eager to get their tree. Decorating the tree was always a special occasion and a "Christmas on the Isthmus" was a popular story. After Christmas, the spruce trees were collected and huge bonfires were held as neighborhood parties around the first of the New Year. Collecting the discarded Christmas trees was a tradition as was the neighborhood bonfire when they would be burned. But part of that tradition was raiding one another's cache of trees for that group's bonfire. Trees were not branded, so you could pilfer an "unprotected pile." Kids slept with their trees to prevent this from happening. The bonfire was a coming together of the neighborhood families, with each family bringing a covered dish. This same tradition continues where Canal Zone retirees live and associate.

Well! Diablo Heights didn't win a lot of kickball games. As a matter of fact we probably lost more games than we played! Doncha know why? That wasn't the point. Nor was it the tally of wins, losses and forfeits. The point was one was on a team playing kickball, which one loved passionately. One awoke with passion. One played with passion. One drank Royal Crown Cola in the afternoon with passion. And when one went to bed one slid between the cool of the sheets to say prayers, to sleep and then to be awakened by the morning sun.

Everyone can learn to kick a kickball. Everyone can kick a kickball. The point is **kickball begins after the kick!** The ball is always put in play. Even if a kicker kicks and misses, flies out or gets thrown out, other base runners can run freely. Running freely around the bases, dodging throws, and sliding into base is fun, especially for the young.

Today, the Canal Zone Society of Florida is an established organization that represents the special interests of those employees who have lived or retired from service in the Canal Zone. Every year around the Fourth of July holiday the Society sponsors a reunion, within which many mini-reunions occur. These mini-reunions are for high school graduating classes, families, special groups (like golfers), Junior College graduating classes and many others. The occasion of class reunions occurs on every fifth anniversary of the class's graduation date. In addition to the annual re-union, the Society publishes a quarterly magazine informing members of the goings on among its members, congress and other matters of interest to retirees. Another special publication of the Society is the issue with all the current addresses of the members. This is a great asset for those wishing to renew ties or see old friends, when travelling in close proximity to their friend's homes.

Chapter #4 cannot be concluded until we truly understand ourselves, until we see ourselves as others see us, until we practice treating others the way we wish to be treated or until we all become angels again! Remember how beautiful our Earth, our planet, looks from outer space? Well each of us looks equally beautiful from the view of the Creator. After all, we are all on the Creator's team anyway! "Pick Me! Pick Me! Thank you, God!"

CHAPTER 5 - THE LEGENDS

This is the last chapter, so if one wants to read more about kickball continue on and then go back to Chapter #1

I am writing Chapter #5 before Chapter #4, because I want to know how this book ends. Maybe "Papa" Hemingway used this writing technique, too, but it's OK if he didn't, because I just wanted to cite his name in my book, before it was finished.

This chapter is about the young people with whom I played kickball and their special gifts. It is an opportunity to share something more than historical or chronological data. It's about us kids. It's about the way we were, because the character traits created during those years of kickball have remained intact when these friends became adults, and 60-year old children. Because they were friends then and presumably would be so today, I'll not reveal their full names. They know and anyone that played against them would know their identity. But I must leave that up to happenstance.

Back in those days at the Diablo gymnasium, there was a two to three foot space before the end walls of the gym where the basketball courts ended. To protect the basketball players a padded mat was hung just behind each basketball backboard and goal. The mat was rectangular in shape, lumpy in looks, about 5' by 7' in size, and had about a foot below it to the floor. I mention this because a fly ball that hits the outfield mat (think of it, a basketball goal in front and above it and lots of kids there to catch the ball) is a **homerun**. See, a homerun is another term released to the world from kickball. It was necessary to mention this because our teammate, one Harold by fictitious name, was astoundingly accurate at kicking that mat in a fly. I could tell it was going to be his intent every time it was his turn to kick. The outfielders knew it too, and changed their positions, moving to "centerfield." (Today in baseball that's called a **shift**. A shift is when the fielders move from their customary positions and overload one side or other of the field.) Harold used several forms of kicks to achieve his goal of kicking homeruns. There was the boomer or a line drive straight at it, this scared younger kids who didn't try to catch it. They really thought the ball would tear them apart if they caught it, or tried to.

Let's write about catching a ball on the fly if one is in the outfield. The line drive kick is coming fast and hard and one has to catch it with the whole body. This is incredibly tricky. One's arms must come around in front like they are going to hug the ball, and one has to tuck in the tummy. All of this has to be timed and done in one movement at impact. If one's arms are too late the tummy, chest and neck all get "tucked" at once, not pleasant. If one's arms come around too soon to embrace the ball they take the brunt of the ball's force. Hopefully after all this pain one managed to hold onto the ball, but unless one times the catch perfectly the ball will just bounce off the chest or carom off the arms. So there is this enfolding of the ball that must occur to catch line drive kicks. Back to Harold.

Sometimes Harold would change his tactics, and send the ball in an arching fly out to centerfield. This is just as pretty as a line drive homerun, but it takes a much more adept kick of the ball. The ball must go around or over the basketball backboard or goal and fall to the back mat in its flight. Most of the time it will hit the basketball backboard or rim, but it is a beauty of a kick when the trajectory succeeds and the ball hits the mat. Now if a ball hits off the back wall of the gym, it is still in play. If one can catch the **rebound** before it hits the floor, the kicker is out, a fly out. If Harold's kick didn't hit the mat, he could easily be out by a rebound catch. To his credit the ball more often than not successfully hit the mat. Today, he must be very successful in business.

Now everyone knows gymnasiums have roofs, but if you look at the roof you can't see it at the Diablo gym. First, there is a bunch of lights. Then there are a bunch of straight lines at all angles, which we called **rafters**. Today, I know that they are the struts in a long span girder, holding up the roof. The girders were placed up there one after another and spaced very close together. If a kick were to hit one of the lights, it was an **automatic out**. If the kick sailed up into the "rafters" and hit one of them, it was deemed **interference** and one would kick again, but with a strike (like a foul ball in baseball), but one could not be given a third strike, as a strike out. If the kickball were to pass through the rafters, and didn't touch anything, the ball was in play. I bring this up because everyone catches a bouncing ball wrong on their shin when they are kicking and the ball sails up into the rafters. That is always done by mistake. But there was our buddy Timmy. He must be an engineer. It is difficult for the kick to pass through all those rafters. But if the kick passes through those rafter spaces, the ball is hard to catch coming straight down off the back wall and that's what Timmy would do.

In the early 1920's, parents wore white clothes and walked. Parading up and down the Prado in Balboa was a prominent activity during the construction and after the opening of the Canal. The Prado was a boulevard running from the Balboa Clubhouse at the base of Sosa Hill to the base of Ancon Hill and the Administration Building. Strolling along the Prado on a Sunday afternoon, was as much a social affair in 1930, as Sunday drives became in the Canal Zone and in the States.

Now Joe, he was not fat, but stocky and could kick hard. Joe was left footed and kicked line drives two feet off the floor all the time. If one were an infielder and one of his kicks was coming at you; forget what I said about timing your arms and tummy tuck. Duck! I have seen so many arms go "whap," which means flung straight out after an attempt to catch the ball. Joe was a serious singles kicker, but he usually got to second, even third base, when the ball caromed off the infielder and went somewhere nobody was positioned. He was always a happy kid! His last name had two "r's" and ended in an "o," so, he probably opened a successful Italian restaurant.

Running the bases was an art. One was inviting the fielders to throw the ball. None did it better than Billy. I could be standing in front of second base and in the base path with the ball, when Billy was rounding first base and coming straight at me. I suppose if one could just hold on to the ball, that would have been best, but he was such an inviting target I would wind up and throw the ball at him, and miss! From the position of where I was when I threw the ball he vanished. He would slide. He would leap. He would contort his body into an "S." It didn't matter, because whatever anyone did, one would miss. Billy was a real challenging, daring type of base runner, and because of his supreme confidence in his ability, by the time one threw the ball, he could dodge it. It was a real thing of beauty to watch him, while the ball goes flying out into space. Knowing him, I would probably say he became a mountain climber and conquered the major peaks of the world or that he became a successful tax accountant.

Throwing at a base runner was an art form, too. None had the rifle arm or intuition of Augie. The real artist does what others can't do and does it better than anyone else will ever do, such as Michelangelo and Augie. Out of nowhere he threw missals, no wind up, just zap, you're out, and it hurt! Most of the time one threw to hit a runner and were satisfied with that. Not Augie! He could hit a runner anywhere he wanted to. His throws were fast and accurate. I've seen his throws knock the legs out from base runners and watched these hapless bodies tumbling through the air, hitting the gym floor, and bouncing off the gym walls, until skidding to a stop. When Augie threw the ball he could curve it to follow the runner, before it hit the runner. That's talent. It reminds me today of heat seeking missals. Why did he put a spin on the ball when he threw it? It hurt more, like it went on grinding into the skin! One really didn't want his throw to hit any of one's scabs. I can't imagine what Augie is doing today, it wouldn't be a preacher, but it would probably be more likely that he became a Medal of Honor recipient.

Julia did it all well and so did Peggy with pigtails and Linda. Perhaps they would have written this book on kickball differently, and used more girls than guys to showcase talent. But they played with the same pleasure as I did, and it would be great to see them today, too. They will probably be mothers, and great mothers at that! All the values learned in kickball make for great parents and grandparents. Let me tell you about Julia. Julia was one of my teammates. She was fast, and good in the field. Most throws come back to the pitcher or infield bouncing. Not Julia's throws. She got to the ball quicker than anyone I knew and could hurl the ball back to the pitcher in the fly. That was as good as most anyone, except for the big kids. I saw her years later, and she was a mother to all sons. I never asked her if they learned to play kickball from her, but I'll wager she did teach them.

There were several special facilities in the Canal Zone such as Morgan Gardens for creating corsages, the Mt. Hope printing plant for all types of certificates, and the ice making plant, but one of the very special facilities was Mindi Dairy. All the milk consumed in the Canal Zone by civilians and military personnel came from Mindi Dairy cows. Drinking milk was as important to the children then as now, to create sound bones and bodies.

One learned in kickball that one had to take as well as give from equally talented kickball players on the other teams, but no one beat our big kid, Jack. He was our pitcher and first kicker; remember why, when I explained that to you earlier? Good sportsmanship was an important lesson. You didn't play kickball with the intent of hurting anyone else; after all, six-year olds were playing too. It was the older kids taking care of younger brothers and sisters.

Daniel G. Winklosky

Being a good kickball player didn't mean one would excel in any other sport and many kickball players got bored with the limitations of the other sports and chose other avenues for their talents. The undisputed greatness of players like Augie, Tommy, Billy and Jack got buried in the likes of little league, intramurals in junior high, and junior and senior varsity sports in high school. High School sports required travel to the "other side" of the Isthmus.

Train trips took one hour to go from Panama to Colon (the other side of the Isthmus) on the Panama Railroad. The railroad was built in the 1850's and some of those old timers were still around for the construction of the Canal itself. The railroad terminal in Balboa was a favorite place to stand and watch the trains come and go. Many people preferred to drive across the Isthmus on the Isthmian Highway at a speed of 40 miles per hour.

Kickball was played daily. There were times though when parents deemed it in one's best interest to travel. I never could enjoy what they thought was "broadening my horizons." An all day trip to Mindi Dairy, where we got our milk, was not fun. Trips to the Tivoli Hotel in Ancon and Washington Hotel in Colon were elegant moments with linen napkins. Other unique places were the Amador Beach for swimming, Summit Gardens for picnicking and horticulture, the Chinese Gardens for fresh fruits and vegetables, and the Thatcher Ferry for a ride across the Canal.

My parents were wonderful people, and I miss them. My older brother and younger sister were great companions and I miss them. That was family and we loved one another. But kickball was my life, and Diablo Heights was my team. Our team was an incredible part of my beingness. One accepted everyone and played every game for fun. Kickball is the granddaddy of all sports. They played it in the olden days in Mexico. All the cultures of the world took a part of it and made it their national sport. So it became cricket in England, soccer in

Europe, baseball in the Americas, and later on basketball in the United States, and track became a worldwide event.

Yet, parents would take trips to broaden the horizons of their children. I did with my sons, Daniel (Gary) and Edward (Ward). I knew they weren't having fun being away from kickball. I had taught them how to play kickball while they were still in the crawling stage. I bought them lots of kickballs and played with them; our "big dog" (who was named "**Whitetail**") played too! Whitetail played remarkably well, even when he was a two-year old puppy. (I kept an eye on him and the kickball, all he got were the old shoes to chew on.) Whitetail reminded me of my "big dog," **Laddie**, which I had when I was six years old. If one drops the ball to the ground it's called a **bounce**. Bouncing the ball in kickball was not encouraged. If one were out there in the field, bouncing the ball, the base runners would continue running the bases and score. If an outfielder was bouncing the ball around before throwing it back into the infield, my dog Laddie came zooming in to steal it away. I guess Laddie and the other big dogs had figured that out and came to enforce that assumption. These bouncer type kickball players obviously went on to become basketball players.

Now there are times when one must bounce the ball. Remember, if there are four playing kickball, one could use ghost runners. Well, one could also play that the runner had to advance by stealth. So, suppose I got on first base. I would have to successfully steal each of the other bases and home plate, before I could kick again. That meant the pitcher would face the runner and bounce (called a **dribble**) the ball as high as he wished to. If the base runner could steal in the interval of the dribble, good! Sometimes the pitcher would toss it up into the air and catch it, called an **air dribble**. Again if the interval were long enough one could steal the next base. Sometimes two players would throw the ball between themselves (called a **pass**) to entice the runner to make a break for the next base, during the interval of the pass. The other alternative would be to just run and dodge the ball when it was thrown. Another alternative game was to eliminate 1st and 3rd bases. Kickers just ran from home plate to second base and back.

Kickball is an important form of play. It can generate the greatest freedom of being a child at play, if kickball is played without adult participation. The exaltation I remember as a child was from playing kickball and those memories were recreated in the writing of "**Pick Me! Pick Me!**" Well, this is the end of my childhood story on kickball.

I bet you probably forgot most of the important stuff on playing kickball in the Canal Zone. One can find more topics about the Canal Zone in Appendix E, and I would suggest reading the Glossary of Proper Names. The pioneers that built the Panama Canal early in the 20th century have the respect of all their fellow employees, because of all the hardships that were endured during the era of construction. Special citations to those individuals and families have been contributed to the Canal Zone Museum. This is important, because the Canal Zone is no longer in existence and there are no longer retirees. The last vision I wish to leave you with is from the Canal Zone. This is the drive along Roosevelt Avenue beneath a canopy of Banyan trees.

RECREATION

The concept of recreation to many equates to amusement and to others it involves participation in athletic games or competitions. There are also social forms of play such as crafts, dance, art, music, or bird watching, to name a few. Creativity can be expressed in recreation. Traditionally, recreation would focus upon teaching skills and perfecting innate abilities through a variety of repetitive activities and programs. To shift the consciousness of individuals requires an interaction in a conscious state with the creative expression. The structures for these interactions have been formalized. They are most often the museums of art, laboratories of technology, classrooms of

The Optimum Soul Environment

advanced theory, and workshops, conferences, sessions, and meetings.

The cyclical repetition of the creative expression is re-creation. The trip to the beach, the visit to the mountains, the travel to historic places, and the personal retreat are efforts at re-creation. These are moments of joyful pleasure, proven from past experiences that generate a sense of well being and renewal of the spirit. When this is not so or the creative expression is removed, wrongly presented, or incorrectly interpreted then the re-creation becomes a ceremony of belief, awaiting revival or awakening, but becoming a limited joyful experience. (See Appendix F on the Joy of Freedom)

COMPETITION

There is a great difference between good sportsmanship and competition. The latter conveys limitation. Limitation conditions individuals to arrange advantages over competitors or one-ups-man-ship. There is little to be said in a positive sense about competition. For one thing limitation is a myth, but if one believes this myth, then competition must eliminate all competitors but one. Efforts that bring disharmony to performers may seem to succeed, but it is a temporary success. The greater result will be reflected in disease of the strident competitors.

The concepts of limitation and competition reflect upon short-term gratification. A word for this mentality is greed. From this source flows all the levels of cruelty, hatred, and destruction of humanity. These are the limitations of spiritless beings. These are the individuals trapped by competition. Who but the winner appears to have satisfaction in competition?

The challenge is not to define a problem or limitation. The challenge is to teach the process of creativity. Creativity in recreation is more likely to have the greatest degree of acceptability. Recreation has become a prominent cultural institution in America and throughout the world. National pastimes are forms of recreation. In participation and audience appeal, the major sporting events account for much of prime time television presentations. Using good sportsmanship messages to the general public would be most easily promoted through the major league sports.

The thrill to be and to exalt should not be removed. The original Olympic games were just that, games or play. The concept of striving for the gold (medal) today contrasts sharply from the award of the "olive wreath." The concept of the olive wreath conveyed the meaning of attaining peace within one's true being, while achieving harmony without. The physical, mental and spiritual aspects of the human nature were all brought into harmonious unity in the performers in those Olympics. There were no limitations in the Olympiad nor should there be today.

Chasing fireflies is another form of play, which exhibits physical, mental and spiritual unity. Whether one child or hundreds of children participate in the chase they are all attaining a harmonious moment of pleasure and share it with each other through smiles and laughter. Such exaltation is to be encouraged. The creative instincts of human beings today should seek such activities and programs.

A **Zen Moment** is self-mastery, becoming one with all things through play. Without seemingly conscious effort the performers create amazing achievements through their actions, resulting in shared exaltation. The skills and abilities of the performers would be mutually reinforced, and the spectators would be witnesses of a dance toward perfection. **Zen String** is just a term of playing racquetball in a different manner. (See description in Appendix G) The objective is self-mastery, becoming one with all things, through play. It is the participant's ability to become one with the court and ball all at one time, while honoring the other participant's similar efforts. Bringing ball and court together in oneness with self, results in play with incredible beauty and skill (luck to others). Without conscious effort, one's play creates a level of exaltation and the amazement for one's actions and achievements. Play at this creative level is unlimited potential for Zen String participants. Child's play is another apt description.

It is not man's nature to survive. It is man's nature to create. Play at the creative level is unlimited potential. All re-creation at the creative level is unlimited. Just remember one thing! We are all on the same team, and the Captain of that team is the Creator; and the Creator is the Big Kid! As soon as this becomes a common belief, the fun and games will begin, creating an optimum place to live and play again.

Daniel G. Winklosky

The Optimum Soul Environment

THE LIGHTS UPON THE HORIZON

DANIEL G. WINKLOSKY

**VIRGINIA BEACH, VIRGINIA
AUGUST 3, 2001**

Daniel G. Winklosky

Dedicated To:

Gary and Ward, My Sons, My Lights
MAJADDAM

THE LIGHTS UPON THE HORIZON

CONTENTS

PREFACE 87
CHAPTER 1 – THE MEANING OF "LIGHT" 90
CHAPTER 2 – CREATION 99
APPENDIX A – SEVEN LEVELS OF SOUL
             CONSCIOUSNESS 128
APPENDIX B – RELATIONSHIPS AND INDIVIDUALITY 131

Daniel G. Winklosky

PREFACE

Everyone is a light, **a spark of Divine Love**. That is our true reality. The reality of what an individual sees, believes and understands is that person's truth; do not judge him! The reality of what others experience with that individual may differ, which become their beliefs and their truths; do not judge them! There is God's reality of these same experiences, which we as individuals cannot comprehend. If God does not judge, who are we to judge one another and ourselves? God has asked us to love one another and ourselves. So be it!

When did you first glimpse a 'Light' upon the horizon? How do you feel when you see the 'Light' at the end of the tunnel? Is there anything about the dark that cannot be fixed by the 'Light?' How much pleasure do you experience when you become aware of the dawn's first "Light" shining in your eyes?

If there are no coincidences, accidents, chance happenings, or random events, then there is meaningfulness for every 'Light' ray that "catches your eyes." Is "Light" not the energy of all life?

It seems that most of the occasions for these experiences with light happen after one comes to the Pit of Despair, or what Saint John of the Cross called "the dark night of the soul." Moving from despair to exaltation is as instantaneous as breathing when the choice is made to "let go and let God."

Most of us can share at least one dramatic event in our lives having to do with light, regardless of the source. Some of the questions above may stimulate your remembrance of one or more of those events. *It would be nice and it would be greatly appreciated, if you would send your own special experiences with the light to me.*

As noted earlier, everyone is **a spark of Divine Love**. The drawing in Appendix D of the human person shows the qualities that sustain life and lead to exaltation in the upper left. The qualities that change our lives, diminish life and lead to the pit of despair and possibly death are in the lower right. Remember everyone is **a spark of Divine Love**. The term used to explain this by Jesus was "I am in you and the Father is in me." This is the Christ consciousness! **Raising the Human Consciousness into a Higher Dimension is what life is all about, not the actions of those who hate.** It is neither about religion nor even about nationalities, because it is about our "human consciousness." There are at least seven levels of soul realization or levels of dimensional awareness. The Drawing in Appendix A illustrates this concept. The **fifth** dimension is a spiritual consciousness, a God consciousness. The **fourth** dimension is the collective consensus as well as the individual mind of man, a consciousness of goodness. The **third** dimension is a consciousness of cause and effect, such as revenge and an eye for an eye.

Those aware of life as a **fifth** dimension know that all life is one, and honor the light of God in all people. Those who have this level of consciousness will direct light energy toward their concern. They cannot act in any other manner and no one should judge them for this understanding. Those aware of life as a **fourth** dimension know that life is precious and believe in goodness and justice. Those who have this level of consciousness may seek a higher consciousness (5th), but will most likely seek justice, and no one should judge them for this understanding. Those aware of life as a **third** dimension know that every cause has an effect, and seek accountability and responsibility. Those who have this level of consciousness may seek a higher consciousness (4th or 5th), but will most likely seek revenge against those responsible, and no one should judge them for this understanding.

The response one chooses will reflect one or more of these basic understandings of reality. **What is important is the**

raising of mankind's consciousness to a higher dimension and thereby having a greater knowledge of God's Will.

It is said that the wicked and unjust will act wickedly and unjustly, but that the good will prevail. It is also said that only the wise will understand. The individual who initiates an action from the 3rd level of consciousness is doing so from his concept of truth, a third dimension reality. Those who observe an individual's actions from a 4th level of consciousness will determine the "goodness" of such an act, which will be made from their concepts of truth, a fourth dimension reality. The act of the individual and the understanding of their peers seeking justice are observed by God, who asks that we not judge one another or ourselves. Rather, **God asks us to love one another**. If one is of this fifth dimension reality, why not seek the **sixth** dimensional reality of God! Always remember the importance of life, and in every **moment** of every day be kind and considerate.

Daniel G. Winklosky

CHAPTER 1 - THE MEANING OF "LIGHT"

Under the Law of the Universe all is one; yet, it is important to understand ideals bring fruition to the life of the individual in the Earth plane. It is important to recognize that Earth is the plane of the third dimension, that the mind of man is the fourth dimension, that the heart of man is the fifth dimension, and that the sixth and seventh dimensions are the spiritual realms. The use of the following terms, as "lights," is to define them and give them a sense of importance, their true significance in the Earth plane.

DIVINE LOVE is THE LIGHT upon the Horizon
Divine Love is unconditional love and the Will of the Creator, the Christ and Light Avatars of the ages. To freely choose to become Divine Love aligns one with the Universal Divine Will to become the expression of Christ Consciousness and unconditional love. Divine Love requires that one's emotions (heart) and attitudes (mind) embrace all of life unconditionally.

> *The vulnerable heart delights in the process of manifesting Divine Love. The path one chooses is sufficient to provide the lessons that lead to understanding. Through these experiential lessons one serves to embrace the passions of life. It is through these experiences that realization comes with the knowledge of who one truly is, that life is eternal, and that Divine Love is all there is.*
>
> *The vulnerable heart feels and senses all that it encounters. It rejoices in all that is harmonious and has compassion for all those who are not at peace. The vulnerable heart will shed tears of joy and tears of sorrow in the process of becoming an expression of Unconditional Love. It is aware of the universality and individuation of all beings, and practices expressing*

acceptance for all things. The vulnerable heart is unaware of its attainment and expression of Divine Love, because Divine Will has gradually become the totality of the person and is seen in all things.

WHITE LIGHT is a Light upon the Horizon

The enlightenment is that period in which the "Light" enters the conscious and physical nature of the individual. It is manifested throughout the ages by the architectural creation and construction of Light Centers (religious centers) for the teaching of such precepts.

If one experiences the White Light, there is a strong measure of hope and well being. There is further openness to the "Light," or a conscious seeking to bring the "Light" into one's everyday experiences. Once one experiences the "Light," an inner knowing can be felt that remains constantly at one's core of being. Having oneness of the "Light" culminates in the perfect life. This is then the culmination of an individual's greatest attainment.

Sunlight is essential for the nourishment of the body. The Light of Creation is essential for the self and is represented by the rainbow, which is symbolic of the earthly journey of life for the soul.

Like a flower in the hand, the soul is its own individual self of beauty and truth. Since the self may be likened to a flower, there is a miracle in the appeal of the flower for its color, aroma, shape and texture. If handed a flower, some individuals will embrace the aroma, while others will enjoy the beauty of the flower, while others, still, will find pleasure in the colors of the flower. Such is the potential of every individual to present their Inner Light for the pleasure of others.

EXALTATION is a Light upon the Horizon
The concept of exaltation is boundless expression and enthusiasm. Exaltation is the sole source of pleasure and gratitude. The runner exalts at the thrill of the air rushing past the ears or the "opening up" of the legs to ever-faster motion. This glee and joy are infectious. Others sense this emotion and "open" themselves to these moments of exaltation. Exaltation does not occur just during the event. It occurs before the event. The participant is awash with emotions of movement and images of excellence in performance. The anticipatory exaltation of the performer is the basis for perfection.

> *There is an inner sense, which is revealed in the performer's countenance. As the event approaches, the individual's joy and pleasure in the participation is at peak emotional conditioning, awaiting the full creative expression. Exaltation does not only occur before or during the event, but after the completion of the performance, as well. The privilege and opportunity to express one's talent is an exalting moment. It is important to experience the exaltation of the shared moment with all the participants. It is certainly one's gratitude to the Creator that reflects the truest form of exaltation.*

WISDOM is a Light upon the Horizon
The existence of the Creator establishes the ultimate truth for the earthly civilizations. Mankind is inherently divine, and the perfect life is part of the natural order of the Creator. From this knowledge the Universal laws and principles are for mankind to know and use. The following anecdotes or vignettes are presented to create parallels between the mind of man and the Mind of the Creator.

> *When a ripe luscious peach is taken and opened, the treasure of the peach is released. The spray of nectar, the waft of aroma, and the taste of peach reflect the treasure in the peach. The dripping of the sweet nectar*

and aroma released from the peach draw the attention of others. Similarly, when a person matures, the treasures of the individual are given. Love, goodness and knowledge reflect the treasure in an individual. These endearing qualities draw others into a bond of trust and respect.

Any individual who would hold a flower in his palm does so naturally with the palm up to the sunlight. This illustrates the natural order of goodness, the flower and the sunlight representing the soul and the Creator. An individual who would turn the palm down toward the ground must drop the flower. This is an illustration that chaos is the willful choice of that individual. It further shows the dormant quality of the self, which sleeps until awakened by the 'light' of the Creator.

LOVE is a Light upon the Horizon

The life of an individual can be represented in five stages of life. These five stages are 'self,' starting with birth through age twelve, 'love' through age twenty-four, 'goodness' through age thirty-six, 'knowledge' through age forty-eight, and 'oneness' through age sixty and the remaining years until death. Looking at one's hand, these five stages can be portrayed as the fingers.

The little finger represents the child, within which resides the ego self. The next finger represents love and is the ring finger of marriage. The middle finger is goodness and is the longest, recording one's many good deeds. The last finger is knowledge and is called the pointer finger, directing one towards truth. Each finger touches it's neighbor to remind one that love is important to self-development and that knowledge is important for goodness. The thumb is unique. It is to remind everyone of oneness and crosses all the other fingers at the same time.

One's hand is a reminder that the perfect life is the Creator's gift to everyone. Civilizations can seek perfection of the self through the five stages of life. Endowed with two hands we are reminded that relationships are important. It is important to link hands and to reach out and touch one another. The helping hand is one of faith, hope and charity. The hand serves as a reminder of the perfect life. One may choose the spiritual path, live the perfect life, and attain oneness with the Creator.

FREE WILL is a Light upon the Horizon

How an individual acts is in direct correlation to the consequences one must accept for those actions. There is an earthly hierarchy of consequences. Those consequences stem from the degree of freedom of choice that an individual has and the "common sense" to act.

At the lowest level there is a sense of bondage, as power dictates the consequences. This is the big bully concept. If one does not do as instructed, then a personal punishment by the "bully" can be expected. The next higher level of freedom is human justice. This is the basis for human experiences, judged by a jury of peers. If one does not abide by the social limitations imposed on all, then a personal punishment to fit the "crime" can be expected.

The human conscious, an internal awareness of truth and rightful deeds, is the next level of personal freedom. This is the ability to discipline oneself, avoiding deeds that would cause others or oneself anguish. The only punishment is the inner anguish of that person for their deeds. The highest level of freedom is the choice to honor the Inner Light of the Divine Creator, within each and every soul.

HARMONY WITHOUT is a Light upon the Horizon
It is the purpose of mankind to achieve harmony with one another, with the environment, and with the spiritual world of the Creator. This responsibility is an inner seed of knowledge in one's soul. Awaiting birth, the self is a part of the Creator, which holds promise or assurance of the reunion in oneness of soul and the Creator.

Given this knowledge, society is possessed with living the life of truth and with aligning with the Creator's will. Coming to an appreciation of this concept, an advanced civilization would prepare for the growth of its citizens. That preparation would be to live the perfect soul life and serve as steward for the earth's natural (geological and biological) existence.

*Periodically, the civilizations of the earth are in harmony one with another and with nature. Similarly, discord occurs periodically. The symbols of civilizations depicting these periods can be easily understood if one accepts the circle to represent the self, which is the mind and body of man. The circle represents the moon in astrology. The dot represents the soul, the Divine Light within every individual and in astrology represents the sun. The circle (**O**) with a dot within can represent periods of peace and harmony. The unformed circle without a dot represents the imperfect self and is represented in astrology as the half moon. An incomplete circle (**C**) and the absence of a dot can then represent periods of discord.*

PEACE WITHIN is a Light upon the Horizon
There is a fundamental experience that explains the essence of all religions, whether past or present. This is an inner experience, the timeless oneness of soul and self with the Creator. This experience is inculcated in the construction of religious edifices by those civilizations. The evidence of the emergence of the "light" into the world's civilizations is represented by the light centers of the world. Though many of

the ancient civilization's structures are in decay and ruin, those light centers were constructed to promote the discovery and growth of the Inner Light in every individual. How one attains to the perfect life became the purpose for those religious centers.

> *A dot, a circle, and a half circle identify the symbols of civilized man's growth to perfection as an individual. The half moon (C) without a dot represents imperfect self and imperfect soul expression. The complete circle (O) without a dot represents the perfect self and imperfect soul expression. The half moon (C) with a dot represents imperfect self, but perfect soul expression. The full circle (O) and dot within represent perfect self and perfect soul expression.*

EVERY ONE is A Light upon the Horizon

Give thought to your name, your family name and the names you are called because of your religion, nationality, ethnic culture, gifts and handicaps. What do they mean? Who are you?

Everyone's truest nature is as a beautiful crystal light spiritual being that envelops the physical body. It is this part of us that the Creator wants us to see in each other. If all could see, how delighted we would be at the discovery of who every one else truly is.

> *The young man was struggling forward on the sidewalk. His head was bowed, but his eyes glanced up from time to time to check his progress along the walk. I saw him for the first time that day, though our paths had crossed many times before that. This was a special day! I had discovered how beautiful the spirit body of every person looked. The young man's legs were metal and his arms were extended to the ground with crutches. He dared not look up conscious how others avoided his eyes or pretended not to see him at all.*

I knew him! I knew his real truth! It made me so happy that I just kept smiling at him. Whenever he looked up, I was approaching him with an ever-growing smile of pleasure at seeing him. He probably didn't believe his eyes, so he would glance up more frequently until finally our eyes were locked together as we passed one another. He was smiling at me because he felt OK! He felt OK to be who he thought he was, but had he truly known how beautiful he truly was would he have ever looked down again?

Lift up your heart and your eyes to this truth, which you really are. Cast your smiles upon each other every **moment** that you have the opportunity to do so. Set your spirit free through your eyes to others. The message in this paragraph is how powerful the feeling "I'm OK!" is when extending it by feeling, word, or deed as "Your OK!" to others. The resulting condition will be the creation of an optimum environment for each person in which to live.

NEW LIFE is a Light upon the Horizon

Every newborn child is a new Light upon the horizon. Each new life is the miracle of the earth plane. The miracle is in the potential that the new life brings to us. The newborn child is a new message, a new revelation, a new discovery, but always fulfillment of an optimum soul for an optimum environment.

The majesty of the eyes of the newborn child reveals their awareness of Divine Love and their remembrance of the light of which they really are. Acknowledge the newborn and encourage every new life to never forget. It is time now to baptize in the Light of the Holy Host.

For the expecting family, create the **family unity circle**, a circle, hip to hip, holding arms around each others waists, which puts the unborn child into the center of the family circle. Come together to form the circle by clapping hands and singing to awaken the unborn child to this event. Bring these new surroundings to the unborn child's attention by announcing to it that the womb has expanded to include more of the family into which it will soon become a member. Someone welcomes the child to the "family;" the same or another person acknowledges the child's commitment to be born, choice of parents, being a child of the Light, and that the child is loved by all of the circle.

Starting to the right of the expectant mother, each individual addresses the unborn child, giving their name and lineage, and any special messages. After the mother of the unborn child gives her lineage and messages, she speaks for the child within her, giving the paternal lineage of the unborn child.

After completing the circle activity, but still maintaining the circle, recite poetry, sing, play music, move in rhythmic motion, or dancing as a group, then clapping hands walk around in a circle, tightening into the center, with the mother at the very center. At this point, let the mother express the physical motions by the child, allow psychics to express the spiritual messages, or other desires.

*Repeat the family circle as many times as "the mother to be" desires such attention to herself and unborn child. The key is to **create a bond of pre-birth love** between extended family members and the child. Create a circle with brothers and sisters, or with youths of the family circle, at "baby showers," or among several expecting mothers, or church members responsible for the baptism ritual and education of the child, but still sing, dance, clap and express thoughts of love to the unborn child.*

CHAPTER 2 - CREATION

IN THE BEGINNING

It is the nature of Man's mind to form **impressions** of the environment and the events, which occur. It is the nature of Man's mind to give substance to those **impressions** through myths and legends. Of these **impressions** the most important event to explain is the beginning of life and the creation of the earth and universe. There are as many creation legends as there are cultures, both past and present.

The mind of Man adjusts these creation theories of life to be more sympathetic with his current culture. The re-telling or re-writing of the myths and legends to attain this revised viewpoint has occurred continuously. The stories of the Older and Newer Testaments have been re-told and even now are revised to make them more understandable in the present.

This process of creating a theory and then centuries later re-creating it has many cultural purposes. The most important is to establish a **link** between the Creator with the individual and his culture. Other purposes of the creation process are **linking** the individual to nature, the individual to his nationality's manifest destiny, the individual to his Divine plan and the individual to the historical presence of his ancestors.

The lesson of **creation** is that every beginning has an end; yet, every end is a beginning, a cycle that is destined to be repeated. The lesson of **religion** is that there is a point at the end of every creation, which requires an affirmation and a judgment. It is for that very **moment** that the consciousness is to prove itself clear and pure.

The lesson of **truth** is that the "Light" within shines forth to be shared with others. The lesson of **Pure Spirit** is that it is absolute, infinite, and the energy of creativity. The lesson of

Physical Matter is that it is the resultant of creativity. When the Mind of God and the mind of Man are in concert there is then the becoming of Man as co-Creator.

CREATION

Everyone at some point in his life honors the concept of creation. To give creative expression as painter, vocalist, guitarist, architect, or sculptor is the obvious method for creative expression. To give creative expression to economics, industrial production, wealth, and prosperity is as easily accomplished. The concept of re-creator or co-creator is not a parallel or divergent concept, but is one and the same.

Creation is a state of unlimited abundance, from a source of unknown origin to some, but from the Universal One to others. The spirit of creativity is attainable. Having attained the spirit of creativity permits one to experience endless powers of imagination. The experience of the creative **moment** is a thrill and delights all that are blessed with it. Having attained such a joy gives one purpose and commitment to express the creativity of the moment. Whatever the moment produced, the creativity process concludes with the expression of it.

The expression is the tangible delight with oneself; and the recording of the **moment** is a service of joy to others. That form of expression can occur in economics, art, science, philosophy, and in any other institution of man, including re-creation.

The labels for creative people have not changed much. The artists and designers are identified as the creative people, scientists as geniuses, philosophers as wise men, and the religious as saints. The purpose of creativity in all areas of endeavor is to shift the conscious awareness of the public. The shift can occur throughout the trade or profession as well as throughout the community or civilization. The shift in consciousness may be instantaneous or require decades or even millennia to be assimilated.

The co-creator and re-creator is truly one and the same aspect of the creative expression. This potential is limitless. Diversity in culture affords opportunities of endless creativity, as does stewardship of the flora, fauna, and mineral realms.

IMPRESSIONS

Creative thoughts are essential for the realization of Impressions. Therefore, if one will visualize or envision the following objectives with compassion, then they will become our new earthly reality. The parenthetical references to a biblical second Genesis (II Genesis) verses are to illustrate the re-creation of the beginnings of **A New Heaven and a New Earth**

Envision a worldwide networking of the Earth's special places in an atmosphere of international goodwill. Although sovereign entities exist, their cumulative historical experience is that sovereignties change over hundreds of years: whereas, the spiritual, historical and geological places have endured for thousands of years. *(II Genesis: Ch.1 - 9,10,11)*

Envision a worldwide network of the migratory paths of the birds, animals, and the mammals and fish of the oceans in an atmosphere of goodwill. National sovereignties exist, but the migratory activities of the beasts of the Serengeti, birds of North America, and mammals and fish of the seas go where nature has led them for countless eons. *(II Genesis: Ch.1 - 21,25)*

Envision a worldwide network of the migration of past civilizations in an atmosphere of international goodwill. Before the existing sovereignties of today, ancient civilizations migrated thousands of miles, establishing cultural heritages along their routes. *(II Genesis: Ch.1 - 27,28)*

To trust in the benevolence of the Earth is a lesson long forgotten. To trust in the benevolence of man for his neighbor is a lesson long forgotten. To trust in the benevolence of one's own self is a lesson long forgotten. These subjective messages have been historically documented, during the golden ages of Mayan, Egyptian, Greek, and American Indian civilizations.

The modern world provides contemporary linking through the Internet, travel, electronic communication, trade, and tourism. These linkages are the rudimentary beginnings of a vast growth in consciousness of man. The at-one-with concept espouses the new philosophy of serving a higher value system. A greater sharing, increased insights, wisdom, and global thinking predominate. The linking of international parks and places, while slow to develop, is the potential source of pleasure for all participants.

The Pax Romana, the Magna Carta, the Declaration of Independence and the Bill of Rights of the American Constitution are the roots of the western world's progress toward goodwill and abundance. Today, the modern version of a Magna Carta is needed to provide the free linking of the world's places and treasures, and to provide linking as an internationally recognized standard accessible to all people.

Raising the consciousness of the world's population to an awareness of international zones brings the entire world closer to man. It develops man's stewardship of the resources of the land and ocean, and of all the animals, birds and marine life.

Man-kindness is a euphemism for mankind and has no limitations. The long-term prospects for the world are better because of linkage consciousness. If abundance has no limitations, and man-kindness has no limitations, then the equation of life on Earth is ideal. Linkage makes the past an important source of knowledge. Linkage makes the present an important resource for wisdom. In the future, linkage will make the Earth safe for all life forms.

The challenge of today is to remove the barriers to linkage. Just as the telegraph preceded telephone, then radio, and television, man will attain international mental and physical mobility to receive the benefits of linkage. Linkage movements by land involve extensive interactions. Linkage by air and sea are international actions, which minimize, reduce, and eliminate sovereign conflict between men and nations.

There are countless opportunities to restore, conserve, and re-create the very foundation of Earth's treasures. Such a developed sense of caring is the initial step needed to enable a world of wants to become a world of prosperity. *(II Genesis: Ch.1 - 29,30)*

DIVINE CONSCIOUSNESS

The writings of the Newer Testament open the consciousness of individuals to a new, higher and happier meaning for life. The Newer Testament writings are about a loving Father, Almighty God, Creator and Maker of Heaven and Earth. This is a marked contrast to a vengeful and punishing Older Testament God.

The Older Testament stories did not show the gentler qualities and characteristics of individuals. Those Older Testament persons should be seen, as we would look upon them as ourselves today. This is not precise but it does show how changes are made a little at a time throughout the ages to accommodate the growth to a higher consciousness in the mind of Man.

The life objective for each individual is to attain the completion of their **heart's desire**. The heart's desire and the **Divine plan** is the same thing, being **God's Will** in action. Two of the most embattled persons from the Older Testament were Samson and the Philistine named Goliath. From the Newer Testament life of Jesus is the story of Lazarus, which occurred during Older Testament times about a young man. Lazarus was exiled from his village for being a leper, because that was the Law for that time. Remember, Jesus said, "I come to fulfill the Law." He also came with mercy and healing to change that aspect of the Law.

In the Bible's Book of **Judges** (Chapters 15 and 16) this episode creates another perception for Samson's power. Divinely inspired by the "light", Samson succeeded splendidly in his service to the Creator in this re-created portrayal of Samson entitled "*I Am THAT Samson*."

> *Just now, at this moment I saw you reach out your hand to put it upon the cool granite stones of the wall. You couldn't see the stones with your eyes, for your eyes were no more. You knew where you were. The room was a cell in the great chamber of the prison of the Philistines and you were their newest and most despised prisoner. The Philistines had long plotted to bring you to this end and now were boastful of their bringing you to this cell through deceit. How was it that this happened to you?*
>
> *Cast out the pain! Look back to yesterday's yesterday and see again the things that came to this moment. The Philistines were unfaithful to the Will of the Creator. The good and just were slain for their beliefs and possessions. None in your entire city or throughout the lands came forth to address the Philistines on these unjust actions. No one was fearless enough to stand up to this evil empire, but one! That was you, wasn't it?*

*In reflection one event seemed unreal. All was a surreal dance caught up in a haze of white light. It was as if time stood still. It was a **moment** when now and infinity merged into forever. Even the muscles of the arm were of another's direction. You stood strong, and in your right hand was the jawbone of an ass.*

How best to explain your true position, above your body, as if a director of a play, directing the arm this way or that, and the movements of your body right or left. No arrow found its mark, or spear or blade took your blood. Those dying men were helpless, almost immobile because of the great energy of the "light" that descended upon the battle. A host of angels enjoined with you and your arm annihilated thousands of Philistines. Your body lacked for nothing and it was strong and tireless through to the end.

You stand now quiet, head bowed and shaven, in a moment of repentance. I saw you pray to your God for forgiveness. You felt that you had not fulfilled your life's mission to Him. I witnessed the "light," as it descended upon you. The heavens had heard and acknowledged your sincerity and filled the room with white light.

Through your third eye you saw all that was within the room and the great chamber beyond and beyond that the palace of the Philistines, where your captors were enjoined in great revelry. You knew their desire to bring you to them for public sport and mocking. At that moment the vision of their destruction came to you. You had become aware in this vision of the weaknesses within the palace columns, saw the points of greatest weakness, and the subsequent destruction of all. The "light" remained with you as the Philistines took you to the palace and chained you to the columns of your choosing. None knew of your strength or plan for their destruction. You knew that as the building fell upon and around you, your body would be destroyed, but knew further that your spirit would ascend at the completion of the destruction of the Philistines.

Girded by "light," your arms encircled the adjacent columns. You felt the strength of your arms crushing the marble of the columns, and then the marble and granite walls of the Palace were no more. Your slaying of thousands of Philistines would become legendary.

But it is time now for the world to come and honor the true life and strength of your character. It was your heart's desire to live simply. All you wished for yourself was to live a life of internal peace and happiness. You desired nothing more from life than to be brother to all, living harmoniously with your neighbors even the Philistines. Your wish was to marry a beautiful woman of integrity, to have many sons and daughters, and to be faithful in all things, especially to your God. Those who knew you well saw a mild, humorous, and innocent part of you. You were in truth a peacemaker.

Few knew how perceptive and intuitive you were, nor did they know about your keen psychic sense and visionary third eye. These gifts were held close within you, because they were the true source of your strength. Girded with the power of the heavens at your right hand was a greater weapon than any army of thousands and thousands of soldiers. History has fallen witness to the belief that your hair was the source of your strength, which it was, as long as you permitted that belief to exist. But let truth be known and let the soul of Samson claim again its spiritual nature. Come forth! Witness to your full faith and power! Declare to the world, "I Am THAT Samson!"

The Will of the Creator is not subject to understanding. Therefore, how His will is implemented is beyond the judgment of history or us, as shown in this next biblical story. The Bible's Book of **I Samuel** (Chapter 17) is re-created, embellished and elaborated upon in the story of David in "**The Gentle Child.**"

For forty days and nights, between the mountain cities of Shochoh and Azekah in the valley of Ephesdammin, was your tent placed. Arising each day and after breakfast, arraying your body with armor, you advanced toward the Israelites and yet again made challenge. As champion of the Philistines you sought to do battle with the best of the Israelites. Upon this morning of the fortieth day, you cried out unto the armies of Israel and said again,

"Why are you come out to set your battle in array? Am not I a Philistine, and you servants of Saul? Choose you a man for you, and let him come down to me...." As the last of your words echoed through the valley, the army of Saul shrank back. You stood for several hours thus then returned to your tent, knowing that the army of Saul would not send a champion forth on this day either.

But Lo! A sound of murmuring is growing, becoming louder from the mountain of the Israelites. To your armor bearer you commanded him, "Go see with thine eyes what manner of noise this is." The bearer went, and was gone a little time. Into your tent he came and said, "Master, a champion for the Israelites enters upon the valley!"

Goliath arrayed himself with armor and with his shield bearer leading the way, moved out upon the plain to witness the champion for the King Saul. You looked about, but saw none advancing in their armor. Where then was their champion and cause for the shouting?

A child! A child was walking through the valley. Surely you thought this is not the cause of the uproar, delivering a child unto me. You watched, actually with great pleasure, to see this youth, his grace of body and limb, and beautiful countenance. No! You have not been here these forty days and forty nights to slay such a one so young! Scare him away lest he come too close to thy sword and spear.

With full measure of breath you shout, your voice booming beyond all the valley and hills, "Go home child! Am I a dog that thou come at me with staves? Be gone! I will give thy flesh unto the fowls of the air and the beasts of the field."

The gentle child lacked not courage, which you admired, as he answered, "You come at me with sword and spear and shield, yet I have none of these, but am clad in the armor of the Light of the Lord of Hosts, the God of the armies of Israel...." You understood well his words and stood and advanced toward the youth, which broke into a run, coming toward you.

Too late! The charging youth with arm circling with a sling let fly a stone, which struck just above your right eye. Dazed you fell to one knee, then sank to all fours as the shadows covered your mind and would not clear. You rolled over upon your back, but still were you dazed, sightless, disoriented unaware of what was happening on that valley that day.

Your thoughts were of another valley in Gath, near the house of your parents, whom you love and cherish to this day. You saw yourself at play with your brothers and sisters, but much larger than the other children. Many mocked you for your big nose, big ears and certainly big feet. It was like that all through your youth. None would leave you at peace for you loved life and *the birds and animals of the valley were your companions. You worked hard for your parents, having the strength and endurance of many men. Soon older youths and men alike would challenge you. Through cunning and deceit they bloodied your youthful body in order to boast of their superiority. You hardened not only in body, but in mind as well, to these activities and taking measure for measure grew too strong for anyone to match you in battle.*

Your wages as a soldier were sent to your family and parents for there was much wealth to claim for yourself upon the battlefield. As had happened many times before, you felt yourself floating above the valley where your body lay and the beautiful child stood over it.

*The Light was all about and around you and you felt you were moving unto the White Light of the heavens and beyond. Your last glimpse of the valley was that of the Golden Light about the gentle child, and in that **moment** your thoughts were how beautiful and honored he was of God.*

Jesus used the story of **Lazarus** to explain how everyone is important to one another. The story further stressed how the Law must change to allow healing and compassion to be extended to all. The Bible's book of **Luke** (Chapter 16: vs. 19-22) is re-created, embellished and elaborated upon in Jesus' story entitled **Blessed Art Thou, Lazarus**.

It was not so long ago. Do you remember your 16th birthday, Lazarus? Life was wonderful. Your family pets were always at your heels ready to run with you. From the time of your youth to your last birthday you were surrounded by the love of your family. It was your hearts desire to become a goldsmith, which would come true when you began your apprenticeship with the village goldsmith.

You can see it to this day, that first pimple upon your thigh. Giving it no thought, you were surprised to find so many in the days following. What was disconcerting was the postule left by the pimple. Your robe covered this attack upon your flesh, until the pimple arose upon your chin. Alas! The proclamation upon you as "unclean" seared your youthful heart.

The Law was the Law, not withstanding your mother and father's love; you were exiled to the village's edge. Your father spoke quietly to you at your departure saying, "Go to the end of the lane of the rich scion and dwell there in the shadows of his refuse. Though I must forsake you, because of the Law, know that thy Creator in Heaven is with you always."

The youth became, as an old man, wasted by lack of medication, food and nourishment. You were reduced to nothing! Yet, Lazarus, I saw how diligent thou were at prayer; how you held all in love; and how you honored your parents with loving thoughts; nor had you despaired of your Creator, even from the shadows.

You knew when your father stood not far away for he would loose the family pets, which came directly to you, kissing your cheeks and licking your sores, expressing to you the compassion your family was forbidden to do. For a time times time and half time you dwelt here and died here in the shadows.

The family pets had raced to you only to discover you were released from the leper's body. Upon hearing the howls of the pets, your father came to where your lifeless body lay, and wrapped it in sackcloth. Along with all the family, your father carried your body to the field of lepers. There your body, your flesh, and all your suffering were buried.

You saw all this from the other side, after the beautiful crystalline angels came to you amidst the White Light. You were feeling an exaltation of joy. The light, the unconditional love, filled your heart. Behold! One in a radiant glow of light said to you, "Lazarus, thou art blessed! Go to the bosom of Abraham." Another, as a glowing golden vision, said, "Lazarus, your name shall be known among all the people." You saw the golden light recede, as it went to meet other sparks of light, just as it had come to you. You knew this Visage of Golden Light, though the world was yet to see Him come unto them.

PROPHECY

The '**Lights**' of History are the familiar prophetic individuals in the Older and Newer Testaments of the Bible, but true too for all other religious books of the world. The individuals were the source of having lived inspired lives and embodied the concepts of knowledge, intuition and prophecy. The individuals described in these **Prophetic References** are Lot's wife, Daniel, Rabbi, and the return of the Messiah.

One prophetic reference in the Bible's Book of **Genesis** (Chapter 19) is the story of **Lot's wife**, whose story is re-created, embellished and elaborated upon in the following "**Ode to a Pillar of Salt**."

You were living in the midst of two worlds. It was your husband's religion that taught the children and provided an environment of peace and love for your family. It was your city which was your home and in the neighboring city where your husband traded that were ravaged by greed, avarice, murder, drunkenness, disease and disorder. Despite the example of your husband to extol the virtues of a man of service to the Will of the Creator, none in the cities were sympathetic and heaped villainous slogans upon your husband.

They dismissed his good deeds and the depravity of the two cities grew more every day.

You saw your home, family and husband threatened by a world outside that became more evil and destructive of spirit and belief in the Creator. It was your husband that announced to you, the children, maids, servants, and his employees that they must leave their homes and flee the cities immediately lest their lives be lost in the destruction ordained by the Creator.

You said goodbye to that world, which had been your home and your city. You took only the clothes upon your back and some food for the day's trip to escape the impending destruction.

You were faithful to your husband these many years, faithful in body, heart and mind. To your husband you brought joy with laughter, love with smiles, and nurturing with the instinct of the earth mother. So, it was a small thing for your husband to say, "Don't look back" for the angels had told him, and you knew you would obey.

You heard the crashing down of walls and towers, the crushing of stone and timber and the unending screams of women and children, dying from the predicted destruction. The Angels of the Creator told your husband that their screams and wailing would be long and heart rendering. To your ears they were, but your eyes were averted just as your husband had commanded of you and all others.

*You felt an uncontrollable rush of compassion for those dying, it swelled and filled your heart and you felt pity. Only wishing to say "God love you" to all those pitiless cries you forgot what your husband had told you and in that **moment** of compassion you turned. Before your* *eyes could see, or your ears could hear, or your voice could speak, or your hand be raised you changed. You had been the jewel of beauty throughout the city and your home. Now you stand mute, sightless and quiet as a pillar of salt. Your husband said look not back lest you become a column of salt. But lo, every column is a pillar of light to the Creator. Thus given such permanence your Light was forever anchored into the world as a column of love.*

Oh, Feminine. How pleased were you to be of service, but you were sad for your husband, Lot, for he was without your love. You now have become aware of the great potential of all people everywhere upon the earth for they could choose to anchor vast columns of light into the earth plane to create a new heaven from the old earth. But you saw how the children of the earth feared their great potential and you were no longer able to speak comforting thoughts and aid them to become their fullest potential. And so, you stand still, even unto this day, mute to the greatest opportunity for all of mankind to be a column of light, uniting heaven and earth with Divine Love.

ODE TO A PILLAR OF SALT
*Come forth, oh, children of mine,
Come close and stand beside me;
See me, oh, children of mine,
This salt pillar of true love is me;
Touch me, oh, children of mine,
See how I smile upon thee;
Shine on, oh, children of mine,
Set your loves and passions free.*

The column of white light anchors into the earth plane, as do other columns of different colors of light. The different colors of the light columns reflect the different forms of energy entering into the earth plane. For example, a green pillar of light energy would anchor and release healing energy into the earth plane. A violet shaft of light energy would anchor and release nurturing love into the earth plane, while the blue light shaft represents knowledge. A column of white light is the light of the Holy Host. A golden pillar of light is that of the Messiah, the Christ, and the Avatar of this closing age.

The presence of these or any other columns of light can be called upon by anyone at any **moment**. The columns of light are the presence and existence of the Creator's energy upon earth. It will be the destiny of the Earth to have had every individual anchor their light into the earth, as a column of their true being.

Another typical prophetic reference is found in the last Chapter in the Bible's Book of **Daniel**. It is embellished, elaborated upon and re-created in the following "**A Vision of the Son of Man**."

I, Daniel, beheld a vision on the 24th of December from the bank of the great river Chidekel. There appeared an angel, standing above the water, clothed in linen and surrounded by a golden light. Of the angel, there was a great beauty and majesty of the body, face, arms and legs, with eyes of great brilliance, a voice of thunderous loudness, and His name was Gabriel.

And I saw and beheld two others in the vision. One stood on this side of the river bank, and the other one (I believed was Elijah, or John the Baptist) stood on that side of the river bank, who asked the man clothed in linen, who was above the waters of the river, "How long to the hidden end?" The man who was clothed in linen, who was above the waters of the river, and who pointed his left hand heavenward, lifted his right hand and pointed to the Life of the World, Micah, or Jesus, known as the Christ and said, "that in time, times time and a half, and upon completion of the fragmenting of the land of the Holy People of Judah, all these shall be finished." The others present felt the enormous energy and cowered into a protective huddle, leaving Daniel to stand alone. Weak from awe and paralyzed by fear, Daniel fell prone upon the ground.

Then did the speaker help me, Daniel, to all fours, and command me to stand, which I did, still trembling. I became reassured by his voice and his words of comfort, and explanation for the purpose for his coming, as Gabriel, released from his heavenly responsibilities by Michael, for this was the **moment** I was to be introduced to the Messiah, and to the end of the present age. And so, he explained the events of the "coming' as by scripture; yet, was I speechless to know of the fulfillment. Then the humanlike shape a'near, on this side of the riverbank, the Messiah touched my lips, touched me, saying, "Go Daniel! The matters are obscured and sealed till the time of the end. Then will there be those who are selected, clarified, and refined. The wicked will act wickedly, but none of the wicked shall understand. But know only that the wise shall understand."

Then the Truth, the heavenly One of Greece, Athena, approached, wherein, Gabriel declared that what He had said was in truth, now verified by Athena. None shall alter the Truth as given by Michael to me, now to you.

After the prophetic vision it is the assumption of the author, that Daniel returned to Jerusalem and set upon the task of rebuilding the Temple, as given to him in his prior visions. Upon completion of the Temple, Daniel returned to Babylon, where he was a retired nobleman of wealth. In accordance to the days of time, being one thousand two hundred and ninety, a great star shown in the sky, heralding the birth of the Messiah, the Anointed One.

Daniel G. Winklosky

With a retinue of wise and knowledgeable men from the synagogue, Daniel set out to attend to the young Prince of the Covenant. There in Bet Lehem, they found the Child and arranged for the travel of the family to safety in Egypt. For a period of time, times time and half a time or thirty two and a half years, the young Prince grew to manhood, traveled, and learned the trade of a carpenter, and became a Rabbi among His people. Entering upon His mission in life, the young Rabbi gave fulfillment to the scriptures and taught for a time, times time and half a time or three and a half years.

A prophecy from the Bible that is fulfilled leads to the greater credibility of prophecy, which seem to be the prophecy of the coming of the Prince of Peace. This prayer is from the Bible's Book of **Luke** (Chapter 11), which is embellished, elaborated upon and re-created in the following "**A Rabbi's Song of Prayer.**"

> *The Rabbi knelt before the golden sunset, the hills low, and the babbling stream, encircling the garden of flowering shrubs and herbs. To any onlookers He would be seen as in deep prayer and meditation. If one stood close enough to Him to hear this simple song of prayer one would hear Him singing it softly to His Creator, and one would be astonished at the joyous melody, which alone could fill the heart and soul with love. The wise knew that the song of prayer was Divinely inspired. Surely, was this Rabbi not Divine, too? It was said that the song of prayer unlocked all the gates of the heavenly universes to be received directly by the Creator. The Rabbi was simply clad in white linen. His favorite being a white robe with golden threads around the collar at the neck, cuffs of the wrists, and hem at the feet. The prayer shawl was draped loosely across the shoulders on this summer's evening. As the Rabbi stood, He motioned to those nearby to come closer to Him. Those who knew the Rabbi well also knew that*

The Optimum Soul Environment

His short song of prayer had been followed by a period of silent meditation.

*He often spoke to these men and women after his meditation. He would talk in His native tongue of Hebrew, but well He knew the languages of Latin, Greek, Egyptian and many others. Those nearby the Rabbi were quick to move close to Him to hear His words and to commit them to memory. This was not a synagogue, but the ground under the feet of the Rabbi was holy ground. All who stood near were reverent. When the young Rabbi spoke, it was as though the ancient wisdom's of all the universes were heard. Though exhausted by the day's travels, healing and sermons, it was truly amazing to feel the Rabbi's peace and love radiate outward in rings of joy to all around Him. The joyful **moment** of silent contemplation that the Rabbi observed in meditation was suddenly loosed upon all about Him in a harmony of love and brotherhood. To the knowing observer there was yet to come the words of assurance, the words that the Creator had given to Him while in meditation.*

*The spoken words came forth, as the Rabbi's voice soothed all within hearing with its healing, compassionate and musical qualities. Neither wind nor blade of grass nor twig nor animal sounded for all men and nature were enraptured within this **moment** heartened by each of the Rabbi's words. Some seemed not to hear and lay upon the ground as if asleep. Others seemed to grow weak and kneel upon the ground. But all heard and all were joyous. The lesson of this day was the divinely inspired Song of Prayer by the Rabbi. To all those about Him, He told them how to sing the song and He explained to them how they were to understand the prayer. Those words still echo through the ages unto the present. Although no longer sung in the melody of the Rabbi, the words raise all those that* *speak and understand them to a higher level of consciousness.*

One will recognize these words and everyone is invited to speak them or sing them unto the Creator. All are opening the gates to all the universes so that everyone may come unto the Creator and learn His will in silent meditation that may become as the Rabbi, one with the Creator and fulfill His will on Earth.

The Rabbi spoke, teaching those with Him how to sing these words and those words were:

Our Father, *which art the Light of all the Universes,*
Hallowed be Thy names,
Thy kingdom come, Thy will be done
on earth *through me,* **as it is in Heaven.**
Give me this day Thy Light *and Thy Manna*
That I may *channel and* **serve others,**
Forgive my sins, and
Forgive the sins of others.
And through wisdom, **lead me not into temptation,**
But deliver me from evil *through understanding,*
For thou art Light, Power,
Glory, Honor and Life Everlasting.
Amen, *Amen and Amen.*

The expectation of the return of the Christ and the fulfillment of the Bible's Book of **Revelations** is the hope of the Christian era. To be present in the world at the time of His return is the Christian's undiminished desire. Since the time of the writing of the Book of **Revelations**, the coming of the Prince of Peace to fulfill the Newer Testament covenant is to be the day of the "great awakening." The coming of the Anointed One will be an event of majestic splendor. The "Holy Host" and all the legions of angels are expected to be present to witness the Messiah.

PROPHETIC FULFILLMENT

The angel of **Revelations** tells us repeatedly that the appearance of the Lord of Lords, Son of Man, Christ, the Anointed One, and the Prince of Peace will be instantaneous. This is the re-creation of the Christ's return based upon the accounts from the Bible's Book of **Revelations** (Chapter 22). *This account occurs in modern times.*

I set down this day the witnessing of the account of the Lord of Lords, the line of David, the Christ and presence of the Anointed One. Surely, this was a day of great and tumultuous Thanksgiving. The great waters of the River of Life flow through and around each and every one of us. The water is fluid and visible, but it is not moist as before. It is the essence of life, satiating all thirst and hunger, but taken without cup or glass or even by a gulp of the mouth. But like a breath of air, the waters fulfill all wants.

The great Tree of Life reached high into the heavens and its branches came low to the ground. It had all manners of fruits. The most delicious tastes from around the world were upon each of the branches. The aromas of the fruits were so pungent that they alone were nourishment to the body. The leaves of the Tree of Life were multi-colored and each color of leaf accorded medicinal benefits to the body.

I live in absolute peace and harmony and dwell in the great City of Jasper, which descended out of the heavens. The angels sang and great cables, or bands of energy, which crackled and sparked until withdrawn, lowered the City upon a hugh foundation that stood between the River of Life and the Tree of Life.

Those who had acted wickedly and unjustly were no more on the earth for their spirits had been withdrawn instantaneously unto the heavens. The light of the Creator filled the hearts and spirits of all who were wise and good, and the light was the same as the white light of those who had witnessed their near death experiences. The light filled each heart with unconditional love and was brighter than all the stars and suns that shown in the heavens.

It was the body that became as heaven on earth fulfilled, the earth remained the earth, but the body became as above so below. Each person shown bright and was seen as crystal light. The auras of every person shown forth in bright colors no longer tainted by curses, sin or evil. It was a transformation, as surely as it was instantaneously done. The joy of every heart was set upon the awareness of the Christ, the Anointed One, fulfilling his return, becoming one with everyone.

The Christ awareness was not seen as with one's eyes, but seen as the mental image of the third eye. One saw a golden light that shown about Him and the music of the spheres was created by metallic ribbons undulating across the heavens and sounded unto the ends of the universe. He came quickly! Just as suddenly as the cloud parts from the sun, He appeared unto the third eye of everyone.

So brilliant was His golden light that all fell where they were the world around upon their knees. His radiance and golden brilliance were unmatched by any sun, yet so absolute was His love that weeping tears of joy and happiness flooded my eyes and the eyes of all those around me. Our visions of His presence were simultaneous as were our release of tears of joy followed by our words, "Praise be to thee, Oh Jesus!"

*Such a welcome, such a **moment** of great Thanksgiving! Oh, joy unmatched! Oh, love Divine! All hail the grace of our Lord, the Christ, who is and shall be forevermore. Peace abided within the soul of every man, woman, and child and every soul was in heavenly bliss. The true home of every soul, the New Eden, the Optimum Soul Environment for all of the Creator's children.*

Amen, Amen and Amen.

Now that is the Optimum Soul Environment! Note the special effects that happened in this prophesy. The lowering of the New Jerusalem (that came down from heaven) with what appeared to be metallic cables charged with electrical energy. The visualization of the Messiah "in what is termed the third eye at the center of the forehead" all perceived this simultaneously world-wide. The withdrawal of life sustaining energy forces from those not witness to the Messiah's coming. The transformation of the human essence, which marries the flesh body to our combined etheric bodies (mental body, heart body, spirit body), fulfilled the words "as above so below" and the "marriage of the bride and groom." Other parallels from the Book of Revelations can be given substance and example. That is not the purpose of this part. The purpose is to show how quickly the change can occur from this flesh world to a more spiritually inclined world.

Daniel G. Winklosky

EPILOG

Did you enjoy the book? What Parts? It is the hope of the author that the reader has identified their level of consciousness, and become aware or can understand another's level of conscious reality. It is through appreciation of what others are striving for in their lifetimes, that each of us can be more sympathetic and compassionate towards them.

I have always wondered why Jesus said, "the poor and hungry shall always be with you." Is there a point in civilization when that ends? Is there a point when there is no disease? Is it to be fulfilled in the promise of Revelation's New Jerusalem? I don't think it has to be fulfilled in that manner. The *tragedy of life* is that the Creator could envelop all of us in White Light instantaneously. The *miracle of life* is that He doesn't, so that we may achieve the New Jerusalem's promise by ourselves. Our tasks begin. May my will be the Will of the Creator. May your will be likewise. May my deeds be reflective of unconditional love and may yours be so too.

Perhaps it is more difficult to be sympathetic to those creating chaos, as mafia, drug dealers, al qaeda, and others that cause changes in life from exaltation to despair and death. It is understood that the wicked will act wickedly and that the unjust will act unjustly. Their actions and deeds are not motivated by unconditional love for all of life everywhere. Everyone is accountable and responsible for the love or chaos that they create in one's lifetime. Everywhere throughout the world there are places in nature of utmost beauty. Some of these are treasures that must be preserved for future generations as international parks, accessible to everyone in the world. Similarly there are historically significant man-made places that should be preserved and where feasible restored. Let these responsible for horrific deeds of chaos redirect their energies and wealth to creating these international parks, funding them, maintaining them, and preserving them.

You and I shall have sufficient challenges in our lifetimes in being or becoming expressions of unconditional love. How one defines tolerance, defines one's level of conscious awareness. How one defines their Optimum Soul Environment is an expression of their belief and faith in a purposeful and intelligent universe, which gives meaning to their life.

How does one create that Optimum Environment for their Soul? Smile! Use these words daily, hourly, and moment by moment – enchantment, joy, happiness, love, kindness. Your soul experiences all of these to the extent of your exaltation. Our soul is the eternal essence of our true being. We have come into the earth reality to be expressive of the Divine Will. We are here to discover our individuality, to rejoice in being who we are, and to learn we are one with all of life on earth.

What about the wait in line for gasoline, work in a meaningless job, stories of gossip and untruth, loss of loved ones to death, witness to greed and corruption, discover infidelities, and all the other "wrongs"? Everything has its purpose for you at the right time. Learn to be patient, find joy even in the meaningless, do what you know to be right and true, honor the memory of our departed loves, express your level of awareness about how others are acting, and know that by example we can change others.

Remember this! The White Light of the Creator is but a moment away in time and thought from entering into your life. Let yourself be continuously thrilled at this prospect. Enjoy your 3rd dimensional reality with the same passion as we did as children, playing kickball and "seeing" everything for the first time. Enjoy your 4th dimensional reality, learning about how, when, what, where, and the why of things and events. Celebrate your understanding of truth, right conduct, and being able to aide and assist others, as mentors and teachers. Enjoy your 5th dimensional reality, experiencing unconditional love for all things. Awake to the power within you to feel compassion and forgiveness. Discover the depths of wisdom, abiding within you. Enjoy all these dimensional realities, as you witness to the world of your spirituality.

Our spirituality is our human essence, which consists of a flesh body and three etheric bodies, making each of us mostly Divine. Our eternal Divine soul experiences each of our human essences, which makes us nearly 100% HOLY. Forget your past injuries and injustices and live in the present moment, which is Holy. Forget any past life Karma of sin or guilt and live in the reflection of the present moment. Draw upon your future life Karma of Holy Perfection. Be aware that our eternal soul is Divine, and every aspect of our human life is like God in action. Now is the time to awake to this potential and be glad.

Allow the manifestations of the universe to serve you! Let your meditations guide you to find the spirit that dwells in all life, the intelligence in all things, even a raindrip, and the revelation of the Will of the Creator. Let your prayers be plainly spoken, but passionately for all, and let your blessings be for the highest good of all. Exalt in all that is, and what can be, knowing the universe of the Creator is meaningful and purposeful.

Finally, know that there is life after earthly death, and that each life at this moment can be transformed into White Light, the Divine Love and Grace of the Christ, our Anointed One. My wish for each of you is that you create your own true optimum soul environment.

Daniel G. Winklosky

BE AN INSPIRATION
Inspire a child and you create a hero.
Inspire a girl and you create a family.
Inspire a boy and you create a community.
Inspire a community and you create a civilization.
Inspire a civilization and you create a higher consciousness.

Is the life you are living an inspiration to another, child, girl, boy, community, civilization, or higher consciousness?

Inspire the higher consciousness and you create heaven on earth.

APPENDIX OF ESSAYS

A. — **7 LEVELS OF SOUL CONSCIOUSNESS** 128
   A DRAWING
B. — **RELATIONSHIPS AND INDIVIDUALITY** 131
C. — **ANALYSIS OF A COFFEE DRIP** 139
   A RESOURCE
D. — **EVERYONE IS A SPARK OF DIVINE LOVE** 143
   A DRAWING
E. — **CANAL ZONE** 146
   GLOSSARY OF PROPER NAMES AND
   TOPICS FOR FURTHER INTEREST
F. — **THE JOY OF FREEDOM** 151
G. — **ZEN STRING** 154
   AN ALTERNATIVE RACQUETBALL GAME
H. — **REFLECTIONS** 156
   MY WORKBOOK TO A HIGHER CONSCIOUSNESS

APPENDIX A

Daniel G Winklosky

SEVEN LEVELS OF SOUL CONSCIOUSNESS

Raising the Human Consciousness into a Higher Dimension is what life is all about. It is neither about religion nor about sovereignties, but it is about every soul experiencing every level of consciousness up to the highest levels of realization. There are seven levels of soul consciousness or levels of dimensional awareness in the Earth plane and there are seven levels of soul consciousnesses below the levels of Earthly consciousness.

Above the Earth's levels of consciousness are the ever-higher consciousnesses of the soul. The **first higher** consciousness above the consciousness of the earth plane is the **Trinity** of Father, Son and Holy Host. Only through Him did the Son of God say how to attain to the Father who is in Heaven. The Drawing on the following page illustrates this concept. A description of the drawing follows with the descent through earthly consciousness.

The **seventh** dimension is the consciousness of Oneness. The **sixth** dimension is a consciousness of an experiential enlightening event. The **fifth** dimension is an emotional consciousness, a consciousness of goodness and Divine Love for all things. The **fourth** dimension is the collective mind, as well as the individual mind of man, a consciousness of compatibility and Human love. The **third** dimension is self-consciousness, an awareness of responsibility for cause and effect such as revenge, or an eye for an eye. The **second** dimension is an embryonic consciousness in that this is the soul of the child in the womb. The **first** dimension is a cellular consciousness, again, a **Trinity** of the souls of the child, mother, and father. This soul consciousness is present before and at conception.

Those aware of life as a **fifth** dimension know that all life is one, and to love the light of God in all people. Those who have this level of consciousness will direct love and light energy toward their concern. They cannot act in any other manner and no one should judge them for this understanding. Those aware of life as a **fourth** dimension know that life is precious and believe in goodness and justice. Those who have this level of consciousness may seek a higher consciousness (5th), but will most likely seek justice, and no one should judge them for this understanding. Those aware of life as a **third** dimension know that every cause has an effect, and seek accountability and responsibility. Those who have this level of consciousness may seek a higher consciousness (4th or 5th), but will most likely seek revenge against those responsible, and no one should judge them for this understanding.

It is said that the wicked and unjust will act wickedly and unjustly, but that the good will prevail. It is also said that only the wise will understand. The individual who initiates an action from the physical level of consciousness is doing so from his concept of truth, a third dimension reality.

Those who observe an individual's actions from a mental level of consciousness will determine the "goodness" of such an act, which will be made from their concepts of truth, a fourth dimension reality. The act of the individual and the understanding of their peers seeking justice are observed by God, who asks that we not judge one another or ourselves. Rather, **God asks us to love one another**. If one is of this fifth dimensional reality, why not seek the **sixth** or **seventh** dimensional reality of God! Always remember the importance of life, and in every **moment** of every day to be kind and considerate, which anchors each individual's light into the Earth plane.

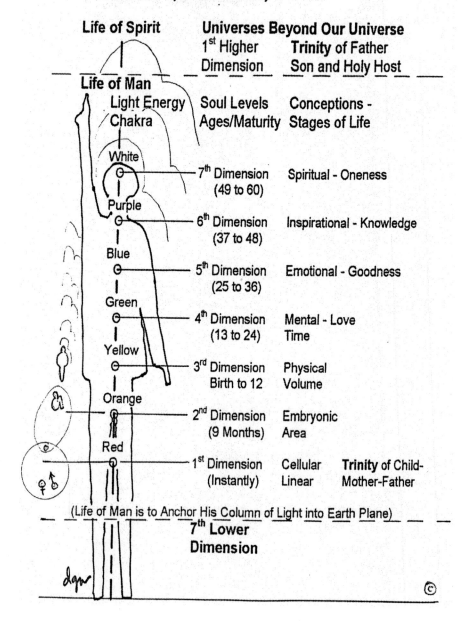

APPENDIX B

Daniel G Winklosky

RELATIONSHIPS AND INDIVIDUALITY

Introduction

During my life, it's events, experiences, education, and relationships have formed my belief system. Every individual has their unique belief system. It is my belief that there is a Creator of this magnificent universe. Aloneness or loneliness is not a quality of my life, as there is always a relationship between a Universal caring and loving intelligence and myself. Given this belief system, the questions - Who am I? What am I? And what purpose is there for my life? - are answerable. The answer to the latter question is to express myself. This generates a question. What or to whom do I express myself? That answer is in my relationships. The hierarchy of relationships will begin with who or which relationship I now consider to be the most important. At the moment of self-expression what counts is that relationship that draws my attention and focus.

Relationships

Relationships are formed from the qualities that we possess as individuals. Those qualities are friendship, respect, trust, love, loyalty, admiration, etc. The quality that is strongest suggests the type of relationship. A respectful relationship would be ideal for student/teacher; a trusting relationship would be ideal for business/partners/clients; and a loving relationship would be ideal for couples/spouses/parents. There are skills and techniques one can use to intensify that quality. Such skills and techniques are available to improve, maintain and contribute to the success of the relationship. The energy of the original quality that defines the relationship is passion. Passion is the desire to be with and share all things in the relationship.

Checklists and guidelines on "How to maintain, improve and enhance relationships" exist in the literary world. A beginning point though is the following "check myself" self-expressions, actions and interactions with others. This is achieved because I receive from others a mirroring of myself. Have these actions been done with a passion for my self-interest or for the other individuals in the relationship?

Do I:
- Maintain eye contact, as there is so much to behold.
- Speak directly to the person to ensure excellence of communication (what and huh means I'm not).
- Ask questions to further explore the self-expressions of others.
- Offer assistance, such as "may I do this" or "get you that" (making others ask for help strains the relationships).
- Come alive when the other party enters the room by comment, eye contact and possibly touch (note military and old southern custom to stand when ranking officer or lady enters).
- Remember that this is true of telephone calls, which means to come alive with genuine "how are you" and "so glad you called." Applies also to email and chat room.
- Remain on guard against comments or actions that "imply" distrust, disdain, thoughtlessness, etc., even if not meant to be so, such comments or actions will be taken, as if they had been meant.
- Know that silence is not a problem, when it is the harmony of quiet reflection about the

The Optimum Soul Environment

relationship. (forced or frozen silence is not conducive to harmony).
- Read the books that foster a philosophy toward better understanding, specific to one's relationships.
- Express my relationships in creative writing, poetry, art, etc., as it strengthens perceptions.
- Know what will hurt the other party and am careful to avoid those hurts.

Am I:
- Considerate, which means doing the unexpected, the little things that mean a lot.
- Complimentary, which sustains the passion and must be genuinely felt to prevent plastic acceptance of others.
- Focused on positives. Everyone has there "down" days, which can be shortened by "upbeat" partner. It doesn't matter if the "down" party just shrugs it off by saying, "You're only trying to make me feel better." Exactly!
- Compassionate, nursing a sick partner is the same as being focused.
- Patient, as all things do come back to you. There is much debate about forcing the issue, better to let it evolve with one's awareness for the growth and self-discovery of the other party.
- Aware that there is no limit to "things" that one can do to "check myself" suffice to say the "biggies" noted above reflect on how actions are received and mirrored back. One cannot predict what relationships may occur, but in a healthy relationship it is important to "feel what" would be the logical response to one's self- expressions.

Observing the relationships of others teaches and informs the observer. Select those conditions that are seen in others to improve our relationships or what we would like to have in our relationships. The family, school, church, job, and recreation are part of the individuals daily opportunities to form relationships. We learn most about life from the opportunities provided to us from our relationships regardless of age.

Relationships form for all sorts of reasons. Some are unhealthy or anti-social. It may become necessary for societies to modify those relationships if an individual cannot. Such societal influence might involve the police. Relationships that are formed may also be terminated. It becomes important that each party to the relationship ensure an honorable termination. When they do not, there is irreparable damage in some form, which may involve the courts of law. Since relationships do cease, one or both parties may have ended a relationship. Even in the best relationships illness and death will bring an end. Following the end of a relationship there is a self-examination period. There should be a healthy rebound, which is inherent in every individual.

Individuality

Individuality is not to be lost in relationships. In fact, if it is lost, the relationship is not appropriate. The growth and self-discovery for each individual in the relationship is essential and is the real purpose of the relationship. We only come to know our true selves through what we learn from the relationship. This is why positive aspects of a society are important, why positive contributions of a religion are important, and why our myths and sagas are important, as they seek to create a wholesome personality for the individual. Without freedom of self-expression, self-discovery and self-discipline individuality is stifled. Never lost, individuality will grow internally, whether transformed, reformed or in some cases enlightened by the sub-consciousness.

Having the freedom to be, to self-discovery, free will and other such concepts, each party of the relationship is witness to the growth of the other party. That growth, maturity, and independence foster positive self-concepts, which are what each party (whether teachers, parents, partners, clergy, spouses, etc.) holds out to the other.

Self-fulfillment of the individual was not the self's goal, but became the result of a healthy relationship. Service to another was the self's goal, but promoted individuality within oneself.

Spiritual Relationships
It may be argued that even after death there is a continuing relationship, where there is the belief of life after death. Though one party is no longer tangible, their afterlife would be a continuation of a learning experience for the surviving party of that relationship. If such is true, then insights into other relationships would follow intuitively. A spiritual relationship such as this would bring profound knowledge to the surviving individual. Such knowledge, applied to everyday relationships would be beneficial in general and in particular ways. The visions or dreams derived from such spiritual relationships would serve to provide a sense of knowing, of well being, and success for the other party. This is a belief system, which is part of our culture. In the play by Charles Dickens's "A Christmas Carol" the audience is presented with such examples. The ghost of Marley and other ghosts appear to Scrooge, making the audience aware of negative actions and a desire for transformation.

There is the probability that relationships also form or exist on higher levels or planes of consciousness. What may be occurring in the physical reality may not be the true purpose for the relationship, if it occurs to foster a relationship in the higher conscious level of experience. This is an esoteric concept, but there is as much likelihood of this happening, as not happening. One is unable to clearly define the higher levels of consciousness, because the words available to describe them are limited. Trying to do so may be commendable, but the degree of success will affect how others will accept or reject the concepts.

Spiritual Individuality

The experience of enlightenment defines the ultimate relationship, a quality of unconditional love between the Creator and the individual. The essence of the spiritual individual consists of several attributes beyond the merely physical. It is difficult to imagine and even more difficult to describe. The most important point is that these attributes are part of everyone. These attributes are who we really are and are the source of our true self-expressions.

The **Physical Body** is not difficult to imagine. This is because it is our being alive and functioning daily to maintain life. Our bodies are easily defined, and by closing our eyes we can imagine what our physical body looks like. We are also familiar with our conscious expressions. This is not as easily done in the following explanations.

The **Mental Body** is an image that is seen as the upper body, from neck to the top of the head. The most prominent feature is the mouth. I say this is the Mental Body because I have seen it in others, when I close my eyes while the presenter is speaking. The words of the Mental Body's "mouthings" are not audible to me but are spoken simultaneously as the words coming out of the mouth of the physical body of the presenter. The person is saying the words of the Mental Body, which I hear physically, while my eyes are closed. The mouth of the presenter's Mental Body is portrayed somewhat "beak-like" and the form of the mental body is somewhat Asian. This has been my experience in all the images of the Mental Body seen to date. The color of the image is a sunburn/red or a brown/red tone. Of importance is that the words of the Mental Body may suddenly not be the same as spoken by the presenter. I asked someone about this and the answer was that the messages coming from the Mental Body may be expressed differently due to the free will of the individual, who is free to change the words and even meaning. Such is the wisdom of the higher self being expressed. I don't know how much better to explain this aspect of the Mental Body.

The **Heart Body** is the seat of unconditional love, and is imaged as the presence of the Christ. This may occur in moments of deep meditation, at healing sessions, despair or near death experiences. The Christ is seen as radiant in a glowing golden light, with a countenance of absolute peace and tranquility, filling the observer with an overflowing of love. The Heart Body is the self's expression of the Christ consciousness with all the compassion of the heavens.

The **Spirit Body** image is of a crystalline shape of exquisite beauty. The individual's Spirit Body is seen as absolute beauty, possessing a sense of tranquility, ethereality, and peace. Unlike anything that would resemble the physical form. The crystalline shape is see-through, though strong profiles and facial aspects are clearly visible. There does not seem to be legs or feet to the Spirit Body, though it drifts freely and easily about. The Spirit Body is the perfection of who we are and what we are. Tranquility and peace are the expressions of our spirit.

The **Soul Body** is eternal. It is the White Light and the image is one of a Spark of Light, the spark of Divine Love. The intelligence of the Soul manifests itself in a manner that is in keeping with the Universal Divine Love, abiding within every aspect of the spiritual individual. Though the bodies of spiritual individuality will cease, there is no death or termination of our Soul Body.

Conclusion

The images presented are of the higher consciousness. With the exception of the physical body these images were created from the subjective part of me. It is this factor that makes my beliefs unique to me. However convincingly stated, these images may not be the same envisioned by others or for that matter a part of another's belief system. How does one find substantive proof for their beliefs? For me, there is a parallel confirmation, which occurs through some relationship, book, magazine or similar source. Since it is my desire to express truthfully, my attention is alert to these confirmations. Non-confirmation does not necessarily negate a belief. Yet I would hold that belief until events or experiences re-shaped my thinking.

Because there will never be a definitive "How to make relationships work," I would conclude with the following question. How can I bring out the best qualities of those in my relationships? I would also encourage smiling. To smile and laugh are the most positive of all affirmations. Ideal relationships are individuals, serving and enriching their lives joyfully together.

APPENDIX C

Daniel G Winklosky

ANALYSIS OF A COFFEE DRIP
A RESOURCE

INTRODUCTION

Probably five years or so ago, I spilled some coffee, "accidentally," upon a writing tablet. After blotting up the coffee, I noticed that the coffee had stained the next five sheets. I've kept these five sheets all this time without purpose! Having written the part about drips, it is apparent that there is a further word or two to be said about drips. This is because I came across those five sheets of paper again, "accidentally," after writing about drips.

Each of the five sheets of paper has two sides, agreed? If there are five sheets with two sides each then there is a total of ten images, agreed? What is interesting, is that the stain on the front is not the exact same shape as the stain on the back of each of the sheets. Close, but they are not identical.

There is something "surreal" involved in all these events. Can it be just a chance happening? Is it too coincidental? How much emphasis would be appropriate to apply to these events? I have to give some credit to the unseen world, the world of metaphysical phenomena, for these events, too.

Imagine these five sheets floating in air one above the other, about two inches apart. Imagine them being arranged largest stain on the bottom to the smallest stain at the top. Imagine that a ray of light shone down from the top through all five sheets. The effect of the five sheets would be like filters, reducing the intensity of the light beam. This is precisely the way the soul experiences the spirit, heart, mind, body and cellular levels of awareness. The earthly experiences result from relationships with people, the animal kingdom, and the mineral and vegetable worlds.

The soul experiences are filtered from the cellular level through body, mind, heart, and spirit. The intensity of the experience is less through each of these aspects of the human being. Love is the most important of all the experiences that is filtered through these aspects of human life. The upward flow is a column of love unique to each individual. The downward flow of energy is a column of Divine Love to every individual.

A "down to earth person" is considered to be someone with a good grasp of the here and now, of the objective world, as it is seen by the eyes, and of the other senses. The "down to earth person" phrase is a bit weird, too, "down" from up where?

ANALYSIS
The following outline represents what factors we have in hand. There was an occasion, it happened as a *drip* (spill), which caused *transmission* (seepage) through layers of paper, making *notations* (stains) upon the sheets, which were *representations* (analogy) of the human condition, giving rise to the *purpose* (meaning) of life itself. It was not necessary to write out a paragraph about these defining words, but it is hoped that the outline provided below will suffice.

The Cellular Conditions/ The Cell - First Awareness Level
- Coffee **drip** through five sheets
- Incident occurred
- Accident that it occurred
- Meaningfulness of drip is important
- Inspiration from going "beyond the physical happening"

The physical existence of the five sheets proves they exist. The next assessment is to make another more concrete statement.

The Physical Conditions/ The Body - Second Awareness Level
- Coffee **transmission** through five sheets
- Rapidity of soaking through quickly
- Density of color filtered through remains as a stain
- Synchronicity of why it happened
- Acceptability for whatever reason

The existence of the coloring (staining) is an essential part of the interest in these events. Because of the coloring, it is important to identify the characteristics of the stain made by the drip.

The Mental Conditions/The Mind - Third Awareness Level
- Coffee **notations** by the five sheets
- Color stays the same
- Sizes of stains vary
- Shapes of the stains vary
- Locations of the stains on lower right corner of each sheet remain the same

What I and others know for sure is the existence of myself, my family, my community, my state, my nation, my world, and the Earth. So, let me make parallels with what I know and also some metaphysical reality to these events.

The Emotional Conditions/The Heart - Fourth Awareness Level
- Coffee **representations** by the five sheets
- Individual life
- Family and friends
- Community and institutions
- Mankind and world community
- Spiritual or beyond that which is physical

Crossing the threshold of a "down to earth person," it becomes necessary to push upward through their physical reality to a metaphysical reality. Finding meaning for the five sheets of paper is a major stretch for all, an inspirational look at these events.

The Spiritual Conditions/ The Spirit - Fifth Awareness Level
- Coffee **purpose** in spilling
- Ownership, my responsibility for the drip
- Freedom, the stain takes any shape
- Truth, one drip influences five sheets
- Purpose, the creative potential is not random

At this point, the creative potential is a series of stages in a design process. The design process consists of five levels or windows to achieve creativity.

The Creative Conditions/The Co-Creator - Sixth Awareness Level
- 1st Level   A Window of **Visibility**
- 2nd Level   A Window of **Awareness**
- 3rd Level   A Window of **Sensation**
- 4th Level   A Window of **Intuition**
- 5th Level   A Window of **Precipitation**

(For more information on the creative process, the author recommends his book on creativity – ***The Pillars of Knowledge****.)*

APPENDIX D

Daniel G Winklosky

EVERYONE IS A SPARK OF DIVINE LOVE

The wave of **Divine Love** enters our lives. **Divine Love** gives rise to life. If Divine Love were withdrawn and since all life is spirit then life would be withdrawn instantaneously, leaving the bodies to return to dust. The unseen **Psychic** and **Cosmic Properties** are the undetected Light and magnetic qualities of the ethereal universe, which gives additional mass to the atomic weights of all the elements and add substance and influence to our thoughts and actions.

Impressions are the thoughts of the human collective mind and the individual mind and are the potential actions, which will manifest as deeds in the reality of the earth plane. Without **air** life can be sustained for a few minutes, without **water** life can be sustained for a few days, and without **food** life can be sustained for a few months **unless** Divine Love intercedes, altering the Laws of Earth and life.

From the separation of God through despair (the dark night of the soul) up to the importuning - "God, if there is a God" - God's Love becomes realized and the spirit of the individual is resurrected. Life, once again, has meaning and purpose. Despair evaporates into the false reality that it represents and is no more!

So, the threats to life are reversible and the chaos that clutters the world is an illusion. Only the truth of Divine Love is real. But the earth plane is the realm of three dimensions, of dualities, and of human experiences. We are to learn to live in this world and to create a new heaven on earth.

Daniel G. Winklosky

Everyone is **a spark of Divine Love**. That is our true human condition. The drawing on the following page of the human person shows the qualities that sustain life leading to the Peak of Exaltation in the upper left. The qualities that change our lives, diminish life and lead to the Pit of Despair and possibly death are shown in the lower right. Remember everyone is **a spark of Divine Love**. The term used to explain this by Jesus was "I am in you and the Father is in me."

The Optimum Soul Environment

EVERYONE IS A SPARK OF DIVINE LOVE
A DRAWING By Daniel Winklosky
God's Love - The Way to the Peak of Exaltation

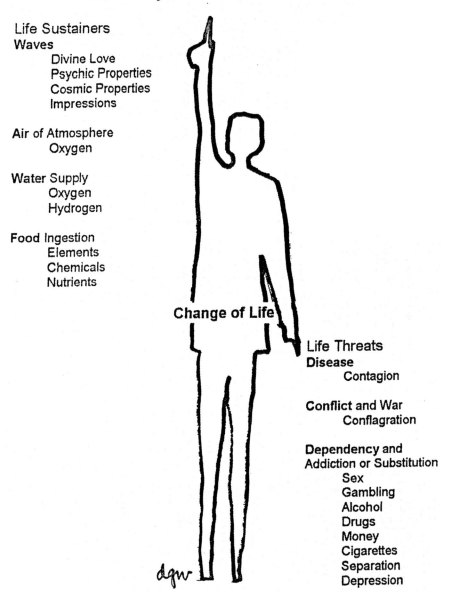

Life Sustainers
Waves
    Divine Love
    Psychic Properties
    Cosmic Properties
    Impressions

Air of Atmosphere
    Oxygen

Water Supply
    Oxygen
    Hydrogen

Food Ingestion
    Elements
    Chemicals
    Nutrients

Change of Life

Life Threats
Disease
    Contagion

Conflict and War
    Conflagration

Dependency and Addiction or Substitution
    Sex
    Gambling
    Alcohol
    Drugs
    Money
    Cigarettes
    Separation
    Depression

The Renewal of Life out of The Pit of Despair With God's Love

APPENDIX E

Daniel G Winklosky

CANAL ZONE

The following descriptions of proper names and subjects from Pick Me! Pick Me! are presented in an informal manner with a humorous intent, as if written by a ten year old. The glossary is presented for further enjoyment, appreciation and awareness of the life and times of the **Golden Era** of kickball in the Canal Zone, specifically Davis Street in Diablo Heights.

GLOSSARY OF PROPER NAMES

Aegeas – A legendary Athenian and excellent kickball player
Al – A Davis Street resident, lived in our four family apartment
Altos de Jesus (Diablo) (See reference to text administration)
America – The land to the west of the Atlantic Ocean
Asian Pacific – The land to the west of the Pacific Ocean
Athens – A legendary place of great thinkers and kickball players
Atlantic Side – Towns of Gatun, Cristobal, Marguerita and Mt. Hope
Augie – A legend among us kids for his throwing ability
Billy – A legend among us kids for his dodging ability
Canal Zone (CZ) (See Panama Canal Zone) – A place to live
Catholic - Another name for a Christian.
Charley Horse – A favorite form of attention getting
Chris – A Davis Street resident, lived three buildings down
Christian - A believer in the Golden Rule
Christmas – Religious Holiday, a time for receiving gifts
Connie – A Davis Street resident lived three buildings down
Daniel (Gary) – My oldest son, played kickball
Danny – Me, the author, and gift recipient at Christmas and birthdays
Dante – A man over thirty and an author of historical note

The Optimum Soul Environment

Darwin – A man over thirty and originator of "Survival of the Fittest"
Davis Street – One of the neighborhoods in Diablo
Diablo Heights (Diablo) (See Altos de Jesus) – My kind of town
Diablo Heights Elementary School – A great place to go for recesses
Doncha know why – An effective teaching tool
Donna – A Davis Street resident lived three buildings down
Dorman – An older kid
Earth – Our planetary blue star, universal home to kickball fans
Eddie – An older kid
Edward (Ward) – My youngest son, played kickball
England – The country that can speak the English language the best
Europe – The land to the east of the Atlantic Ocean
God (Creator) (Big Kid) – Omnipresent essence
Golden Rule - The true meaning of good sportsmanship
Greece (Old World) – The ancient times of the Olympics
Greek – Mythical gods/goddesses playing kickball on Mt. Olympus
Gresham – A man over thirty, noted for economic statements
Harold – A legend among us kids for his homeruns
Heads Up – An attention getting action or phrase
Hemingway, "Papa" – An author of extraordinary note
Herbie – An older kid
Hercules – A legendary Spartan and superior homerun kicker
I Pick You – Almost as wonderful, as hearing *I Love You*!
India – The home of really different religious concepts
Jack – A big kid, and my brother
Jesus – A Big Kid, too! He played in a tough neighborhood
Joe – A legend among us kids for his kicking ability
Johnny – A Davis Street resident lived two buildings down
Julia – A legend among us kids for her fielding ability
Keds – Black high top and white low cut tennis shoes we wore
Korea – The Land of the Morning Calm
Korean Herald – A newspaper in the Land of the Morning Calm
Laddie – My big dog that played during our neighborhood games

Laffer – A man over thirty, noted for an economic curve
Linda – A Davis Street resident lived across from our building
Lombardi, Vince (See reference to text remark)
London – The city where it is difficult to understand spoken English
Luis – An older kid
Mary – A Davis Street resident lived three buildings down
Mary Ann – My sister and princess
Medal of Honor – The real life champions!
Mexico – A land of ancient shrines, pyramids, and kickball stadiums
Michelangelo – A legendary artist, quit playing kickball to paint
Mindi Dairy – An all day trip to see the home of cows
Miss Brown - Teacher (See reference to third grade)
Mom and Dad – My parents, very patient too, MAJADDAM
Mousetrap (See reference to dramatic production)
Mrs. Brooks – Teacher (See reference to third grade)
Mrs. Wright – Teacher (See reference to fourth grade)
Nirvana – A place or state of being, involving white light
Olympian – A major type of athlete, competed for an olive branch
Oprah – A woman over thirty, who has not lost her kickball values
Owen – An older kid
Pacific Side – Towns of Balboa, Ancon, Pedro Miguel and Gamboa
Panama – A Land Divided and a World United
Panama Canal Zone (CZ) (See reference to text administration)
Panama City – Situated next to the CZ, but only adults could go there
Paul – A Davis Street resident lived three buildings down
Peggy – A Davis Street resident lived two buildings down
Plato – A man over thirty, but noted for his good thinking skills
Protestant – Another name for a Christian
Ray – An older kid
Republic, The – The first published rule book on kickball
Roger – A Davis Street resident lived all the way down
Ronnie – An older kid

The Optimum Soul Environment

Royal Crown Cola (See reference to text economics)
Shakespeare – A Legendary versifier, wrote about kickball's virtues
Smith, Adam – A man over thirty, good observer of life's activities
Timmy – An older kid
Tinker – An older kid
Tomboy – Applies only to girls who were playing kickball
Tommy – A Davis Street resident lived two buildings down
Union Church – A place to keep really young kids on Sundays
United States of America (USA) – The magic land to the north
Viagra – A potent cocktale
Wheaties (See reference to text advertisement)
Whitetail – My sons' big dog
Win – A nickname was one of many, like Wink and spider
Winklosky – My father's family name, which was really Vinclefsky
WW II – Abbreviation for World War Two, a painful time!
Zen – A mysterious religion of the very far-east

FOR FURTHER INTEREST, RESEARCH, AND APPRECIATION

The following subjects have been presented in the text with minimal explanation. For the reader's further appreciation and awareness of the life and times of that **golden era** in Diablo Heights, Canal Zone, suggested topics are listed below.

TOPICS

Administration Building
Ancon Hill
Barro Colorado
Carnival
Chinese Gardens
Clubhouse
Colon
DDT
Ferdinand De Lesssep

Amador Beach
Balboa
Canal Zone Society of Florida
Chagras River
Chiva
Colombia
Darien
Egypt
French Canal Commission

Daniel G. Winklosky

Gatun Lake
Goethals
Isthmus of Panama
Morgan Gardens
Panama Canal Commission
Pedro Miguel Locks
Royal Palm Tree
Suez Canal
Thatcher Ferry
Theodore Roosevelt
Washington Hotel

Gatun Locks
Gorgas
Miraflores Locks
Mt. Hope Printing Plant
Panama Railraod
Prado
Sosa Hill
Summit Gardens
Thatcher Ferry Bridge
Tivoli Hotel
Zonian

APPENDIX F

Daniel G. Winklosky

THE JOY OF FREEDOM

Let **the Joy of Freedom** ring throughout the world. There is no perfect peace, except that which one claims within oneself, nor is there any perfect freedom unless it is true for all. It is the mystery of the Universe that there is a Divine Will and that the Divine Will grants to individuals everywhere on earth a freedom of individual will.

> *"Harken all ye nations and kings, rulers and governors for children are heir to inner peace and harmony without. Let the earth shake and dismantle vanity, let the seas swell and swallow greed, let the winds gale and vanquish ignorance, and let the sunshine bring forth righteousness upon the lands."*

The freedom of individual will is the gift of a benevolent power. All others that usurp that premise deny individual freedoms. There is less freedom in the United States today than there was fifty or twenty years ago. However, there is no less freedom for each individual to exercise their Divinely given free will to attain inner peace. Bringing understanding into a world of human chaos seeks to identify the sources of chaos and to mitigate that chaos. Bringing compassion into a world of human suffering seeks to eliminate the sources for that pain and suffering. If wisdom dominates the ruling powers that be, there is enlightenment within that culture. Though that culture would not be perfect because human suffering and poverty are lessons in themselves, such cultures can be instrumental in achieving inner peace for individuals and a harmony throughout the culture. Even if one were not to acknowledge a higher source or heavenly Creator, the culture would serve itself and its citizens. These were the Greek cultures of the ancient world. Their philosophers were seeking "to give perfection of individuality and harmony to all things" a political basis for stability. Their efforts were laudable and many such philosophies did accept and acknowledge a hierarchy of godly beings.

It is in modern society that these political alternatives have produced more chaos than harmony and more suffering than peace. The written history of the western heritage from ancient times to the present has been a long period of trial and error for that absolute political system. None have worked, though limited government seems to work better than others. Only those societies that appear to have no structure seem to have success, such as the nomadic aborigines of Australia. This is hearsay, for I have not witnessed this culture, except through the written words of another. Life does demand individual perfection of our talents and gifts. However defined, there are many differences in all of us, and in those qualities that give diversity and beauty to every culture. Perhaps one culture can teach one thing and do one thing better than any other culture, and that's good. The same is true for individuals.

What kind of political equation does it take to allow these special talents to emerge in an individual and in a culture? The answer to that equation is the ability of the individual to freely express his gifts, and for a society to freely allow advancement in all its expressions. If a God were a determining factor in this equation, it would have to be through **assurances** that all individuals would be free to develop and express their gifts within their cultures. It might also be construed that a God would have to **provide** the gifts to those individuals.

The **Joy of Freedom** is an exhilaration of majestic proportions and causes all that experience such joy to seek to recreate it over and over throughout their lifetime. Many seek simple pleasures, others seek thrills beyond the limits of safety, while others seek substances to provide the feeling of freedom. The perfection of the individual is the ability to find the joy of inner peace through the free will of one's spirit. It hinges not on others or cultural freedoms or political systems, but in a belief system of an eternal life. How one gets to that point in life is one of the incredible parts of the journey through life. It is a milestone in belief to have an event of such an assurance. Faith and belief may serve the individual well and indeed it does for a majority of the people.

APPENDIX G

Daniel G. Winklosky

ZEN STRING

AN ALTERNATIVE RACQUETBALL GAME

Every individual is a pair of opposing internal forces or vortices, twin tornadoes. A geometric shape represents the pair of tornadoes, which are a pair of vibrations, each pattern unique to every individual and to the mood of that individual. These energies may be like two overlapping equilateral triangles, which are most harmonious when centered, creating a star shape pattern. At the point of rage or uncontrolled anger the two triangles close tip to tip to form an hour glass pattern. Even a relatively quiet person in appearance may have created an hour glass pattern and a volcanic eruption is certain, awaiting only a spark to set it off. It is this energy pattern which requires considerable self-control. Avoiding this energy vortex is important for the safety of all upon the racquetball court. It is rare that individuals would be capable of holding the energy vortices tip to tip without rage. The vortex pattern of highest energy output is the diamond shape, consciously setting the vortices base to base. Only through the release of the vortex energies, base to base, can one be masterful in Zen String. It is to let go of one's consciousness and become one with all things. The exultation is to be found in one's skills and abilities to master the ball within the court. What usually happens on the racquetball court is influenced most by the energy vortices of the participants during play. Subtle energies are created by natural vibration rates of the ball and court. Zen String provides for each individual to serve five (5) volleys apiece then side out. The play should continue with seven service exchanges. Each player seeks self-mastery and spectators are witnesses to a **dance** toward perfection.

The Optimum Soul Environment

ZEN STRING

AN ALTERNATIVE RACQUETBALL GAME

Daniel G Winklosky

RACQUETBALL IS AS EASY AS 1 - 2 - 3

1	2	3
UNITY	**RULES OF PLAY**	**LEVELS OF PLAY**
Oneness	Safety of all players	Recreation
	Play by the rules	Conditioning
		Self-mastery

1	2	3
POSITIONING	**ADDRESS THE BALL**	**TYPES OF SERVES**
Center court	Racquet head up	Power
	Step into shot	Lob
		"Z"

1	2	3
ANTICIPATION	**BACKWALL PLAY**	**TYPES OF VOLLEYS**
Prepare for shot	Allow ball to go to wall	Floor to knee
by opponent	Strike ball to back wall	Knee to chest
		Chest and above

1	2	3
CONCENTRATE	**REPLAYS**	**PARTS OF A GAME**
Keep eye on ball	Hinders	Five volleys each
(Forget last shot)	Screens	Seven sets of volleys
		Perfect Shot & Dance

APPENDIX H

Daniel G. Winklosky

REFLECTIONS

MY WORKBOOK TO A HIGHER CONSCIOUSNESS

WORKBOOK INTRODUCTION

Everyone's life is about changing and growing. Life challenges us to discover who we are. We are what we believe and that is how we live. Everyone can see how we change from children, to become teens, then young adults, adults and finally old timers. Throughout this maturing process, there is the joy of becoming strong and wiser and overcoming the difficulties and challenges everyone faces. Just as there are levels of awareness in the physical self's growing up, there are also levels of awareness in love, service, knowledge, and spirituality. These are the areas addressed in **Reflections**. Work through the seven suggested exercises. There is no time limit for completion. Grading is not an issue. There are no right or wrong choices or expressions. It is suggested that you fully understand the material presented in each lesson before going to the next.

*The first lesson is a parallel passage, a parable of sorts, between seven levels of math awareness and the seven levels of conscious awareness, described throughout this book. The second lesson is taken from the Bible and identifies the apostle Simon-Peter's seven levels of awareness. The third lesson is an exercise in releasing to the imagination through visualization. This is a foundation before releasing to a meditation, which is the sixth lesson. The fourth lesson is man's stages of life and the fifth lesson is to understand the human essence of each and every life. The seventh lesson is a suggested journal of dreams, visions, and angelic appearances. This will provide a basis for understanding where one's level of conscious awareness is at that **moment**.*

EXERCISE –1   THE MATH LESSON
The sixth grader gave his explanation about what math was to the senior high school math student. The senior understood and knew that the sixth grader's awareness of math was true. The senior also knew that there was more to math than that. In fact the senior gave his explanation of what math was to the college math major. The college math major understood and knew that the senior math student's awareness of math was true. The college math major also knew that there was more to math than that.   In fact the college math major gave his explanation of what math was to Einstein. Einstein understood and knew the college math major's awareness of math was true. Einstein also knew that there was more to math than that. In fact Einstein gave his explanation of what math was to the Archangel Michael. Michael understood Einstein's awareness of math was true. Michael also knew that there was more to math than that. In fact he was aware of a Universal knowledge of math to be gained from the Universal Teacher. It was the Universal Teacher who had taught him, just as he had taught Einstein, who had taught the college math major, who in turn had taught the high school senior, who had taught the sixth grader.

Create a scenario of understanding similar to the "math" lesson, by substituting the word "Holy." Perhaps you might consider the spelling of the word a little differently at each level of awareness, such as holy, Holy, HOLY, H-O-L-Y, and finally E-LO-HIM (Y-L-O-H).

If you were to select an area of your life that was important to you at this time, what would it be? Can you see how you have grown through the years in that area? Can you identify the major turning points or changes in beliefs and at what age? Ask yourself which level of awareness you are at, and if you are to continue growing in this area what do you have to do next? What resources do you have to assist you to go beyond your present beliefs?

EXERCISE #2   THE BIBLICAL LESSON   (Luke Ch.5:4-9)
In this scenario Jesus suggests to Simon to cast his net in deeper water. Simon answered Jesus by saying that he had fished there all night and had not caught anything, but agreed to do so. Having done so, Simon's net became so full it began to break and he signaled for his partners in the other boat to come to his aide. Then both boats filled so full that they began to sink, but made it back to shore before that could happen. At this point in the story Simon falls on his knees before Jesus and tells Jesus to leave him for he was a sinful man. He and all his companions were astonished at the catch of fish. At this point Jesus told Simon not to be afraid and that in the future he would make him a fisher of men.

Consider that Simon's first response to Jesus was that he felt sure there were no fish there to be caught. This is the 3rd dimensional reality of cause and effect of fishing all-night and catching nothing. Simon was overjoyed at the catch, but alarmed that the net would break, a 3rd dimensional reality. Simon felt an assurance that his partners would come to his aid when he called them, a 4th dimensional knowing. Knowing that having the two boatloads of fish would provide ample food and income for all their families for quite a while, Simon felt remorse for his lack of trust in Jesus, a 4th dimensional reality. The 5th dimensional reality was attained, when Simon felt the love of Jesus was wasted on him. Simon confessed to Jesus that he was a sinful man and unworthy of being in Jesus' presence. This was the 5th dimensional reality, Jesus' unconditional love and an awakening to the Christ consciousness in Simon. At this point Jesus prepared Simon for the 6th dimensional reality, saying that he would become a fisher of men's spirits.

The Optimum Soul Environment

EXERCISE #3   THE VISUALIZATION LESSON
Find a comfortable position, sitting or lying down, to allow yourself to create a visualization, an imaginary place to visit. Relaxing all your muscles, put yourself into an attitude of being at peace within and without. A sample visualization follows, which you may tape or use to further your visualization experiences. Begin your visualization.

Let your feet relax. Feel the relaxation moving up your legs, through your torso and along your arms and hands. Feel your shoulders relax and all the tension release from your neck. Breathe deeply, again and again and feel the release of all emotions from your face and mind. In your mind see yourself standing in the middle of a meadow of wild flowers where the sea of yellow blooms sway and move to the breeze, as it brushes past your face and cools your cheeks. Put your attention upon the flowers. Observe the numerous honeybees at work and butterflies, wafting across the flowers. Listen to their efforts. The sounds are surprisingly melodic. Feel the joy and pleasure arising within you that is awakened by this place. Your powers of sight and sound astonish you. You find yourself totally enthralled by every little detail and how meaningful it all is. You are aware of a sense of oneness that you have with all things and how much unconditional love you feel for all that is. Rays of the sun burst from the clouds and spotlight your space. This is too real to be by chance. You reflect upon this and know intuitively that you have a greater purpose and meaning in life. Begin now to return from your visualization into your room. Feel the weight of your body and sense the smells and sounds around you. Breathe deeply, again and again and open your eyes when you are ready. Do you return with detachment, a sense of peace, happiness, even an abiding love for everything?

Whether your visualization, or the one written above, do you recall your emotions? Did you pay attention to details? Start with the details and list them in the order they appeared to you. Following your writing of these details, create a second list identifying the emotions evoked by them as they occurred. You were transforming yourself through this exercise. Repeated visualizations will develop greater remembrance of details and intensify your emotions.

DATE _____

VISUALIZATION EXPERIENCE _____

LIST OF DETAILS RECALLED:

_____

_____

_____

_____

LIST OF EMOTIONS FELT:

_____

_____

_____

_____

The Optimum Soul Environment

EXERCISE #4   THE LIFE LESSON
Our levels of awareness or dimensional realities are witnessed at each major change in our lives from babes to adults. Within each of these "stages" of growth, all the levels of awareness can and usually are attained. To give some definition to these "stages" a period of time is provided. The first period is from a babe to 12 years of age. Then every twelve years completes another period until death. Birth and death are two significant events, but are not a part of the five "stages." The titles for the five stages of twelve year intervals from birth are SELF, LOVE, GOODNESS, KNOWLEDGE AND ONENESS until death. Within each of these stages, one may experience some measure of all of them - self, love, goodness, knowledge and oneness. Every "stage" is important for the development of that particular intrinsic value, such as GOODNESS by age 48. As indicated by the title, these words define the potential of a dimensional reality. SELF is the 2nd dimensional reality. LOVE is the 3rd dimensional reality. GOODNESS is the 4th dimensional reality. KNOWLEDGE is the 5th dimensional reality and ONENESS is the 6th dimensional reality. Look back over your lifetime and consider your experiences during these "stages." Even though you have not considered them important as time periods, do so now.

Start with a grid on a sheet of paper, as shown at the end of this exercise, heading the columns across the top with the titles of the five stages in capital letters. Although you may not be as old as many of these columns, these stages await you. To the far left create another column of these same titles but in lower case. To the best of your remembrances, begin putting words under these headings. Keep this as part of your journal, entering words which reflect your first awareness of a part of your life's beliefs, and your effect upon others. Continuing, identify those words that created the greatest joy in your life or gave you the most peace. What would you define your level of awareness to be at those times? For example, winning a golf tournament at age 48 would be placed under the heading of KNOWLEDGE, and would also be entered under **self** in the horizontal. Where would you put the word "discipline" and "practice" in this example? Maintain your journal for several years. After each succeeding year, review the lessons and determine what key lesson was created for you to experience that year.

STAGES OF LIFE'S LESSONS

STAGE	SELF (0-12)	LOVE (13-24)	GOODNESS (25-36)	KNOWLEDGE (37-48)	ONENESS (49-100)
self					
love					
goodness					
knowledge					
oneness					

EXERCISE #5   THE HUMAN LESSON

It has been said that man is both flesh and spirit. Therefore, man is admonished to serve either flesh or spirit. Serving both would not be possible. When a man becomes a student, learning becomes his choice. What would be your choice at this moment between flesh and spirit? What would it take to make you committed to serving the spirit? Read the following description of being human and having an eternal Soul. Will you ever learn not to worry about making the wrong choice?

The Bible asks those who have eyes to see and those who have ears to hear to look and hear not of the worldly things but of the spiritual things. The Bible urges everyone to love the LORD with body, mind, heart and spirit, though perhaps not as you might think. Let me explain what there is to see and what there is to hear in terms of our human essence. In addition to our physical body we each possess a mental body, heart body, spirit body and our eternal Soul body. Is this not wondrous news?

As explained in Appendix B, the Soul dwells in each of the human concepts of "body." The existence of the mental body is given to us in the Book of Acts, when at Pentecost, the fiery tongues sat upon the 12 disciples. Each disciple was speaking in tongue and the mental body, which was visible as a flaming tongue, was guiding the words of the disciple. Yes this is difficult to describe and believe. An example of the heart body is seen as the golden glow or aura about the figures of Biblical history. They are portrayed as having the Christ's indwelling unconditional love and in fact manifest it with a beauty of serenity. Examples of the spirit body are more frequent and are noted in the Bible, when the individual is carried away in spirit form to another higher place.

The human being is far more complex than you imagined, and far more Holy than most believe. The mental body speaks to us from the Holy Spirit. The heart body envelops all of us in the Christ consciousness. The spirit body is the "etheric vehicle" that takes us in spirit form to the foot of the Throne of God. There is no sin, impurity, or unholiness attached to these essences of which we are.

Be patient with yourself in your human physical body, your thoughts, your emotions and your concepts of guilt. Think first upon the concept of how truly Holy you really are. Think of yourself as always being a **moment** away from receiving the Holy Spirit, such as at Pentecost.

Practice your beliefs, and grow into a greater appreciation for that which you truly are. Let your imagination consider these essences of yourself and what potential you have for creating heaven on earth, and your optimum soul environment. Would you desire anything else now that you know who and what you truly are? Go! Create! Serve one another! Love one another! And come before the presence of God with thanksgiving!

Exercise #6 THE MEDITATION LESSON

To prepare you for a meditation it was necessary to develop your ability to visualize. It was necessary for you to understand the human essences and the presence of life's stages in your life. Finally it was necessary to prepare you for lessons that come to us when we are ready for them.

Take a comfortable position and begin to relax your muscles and release your thoughts, attitudes, and concerns. Aware now of your physical body, breathe deeply but slowly, concentrating on releasing from your body, and in leaving it honor it and hold it secure for your return to it. Move now into your mental body, feel this Holy sanctuary of truth and wisdom, which acknowledged by you or not, it gives to you daily. Honor you mental body and leaving it love it and hold it secure for your return to it. Move now into your heart body, feel the total acceptance and love that gives you Christ's presence and His consciousness. Honor your heart body and leaving it bless it and hold it secure for your return to it. Move next into the spirit body, feel the sensation of absolute freedom and oneness with the Divine. Honor your spirit body and be patient, awaiting the messenger of the heavens to assist you in understanding God's Will for you. Allow the silence of the moment to expand within you creating a sense of eternity.

When you are ready to release your spirit body do so with love and appreciation. Returning to your heart body, release it also with love and compassion. Return to your mental body and release it with reverence and appreciation. Now return to your physical body and acknowledge it, feeling love and gratification for it's existence.

Practice this experience to pursue your heart's desire, clarify your life's mission, and/or seek the presence of the Christ or God.

EXERCISE #7 THE JOURNAL LESSON

Whenever we have a dream, unusual event, chance happening or spiritual enlightenment that is an important **moment**. These moments should be documented and detailed as to time and date of occurrence. We are all subject to forgetfulness, so it is important to make the notations as quickly as possible in the journal, or upon slips of paper to transfer to the journal. Timely entries or the discipline to write them down will be the primary difficulty encountered.

Everyone has up and down cycles in relationships, work, recreation, and spiritual consciousness. These are the subjects of the dreams, visions, and moments of insight. By creating and maintaining a journal of these moments we become more observant and our awareness of our higher consciousness is heightened.

Just as you maintain a ledger of daily expenses and summarize them weekly or monthly into broad categories, the same should be true for you to categorize the moments into the appropriate "stage" titles (self. love, etc.). Your effort to journal your experiential moments will have it's rewards. The most important consequence of this effort will be a heightened sense of expectation - "Woopie, what's next?" Living in a state of expectation is your reward.

SELF-EXPRESSION

Expression of the "ego" is the same concept as the expression of the "self." *Self-expression* is appropriate for every age of your lifetime. The expression of self is the most significant aspect of one's level of awareness. In the formative years of a child's growing up, the purpose of growth should be to attain a sense of **self-consciousness**. Through the first twelve years each child is attempting to identify it's self, or find, or discover who they are. This creates a sense of reality or a level of awareness of one's self, family, education and environment. Finding a sense of self, the child moves through the next twelve years as a teenager/young adult, seeking a place among his peers, family, school, church and neighborhood or town. This period of a young adult's growth should be guided by **self-discipline**. Once learned, self-discipline becomes a stepping stone into the adult future.

After about age twenty-five, an adult should develop **self-motivation**, which creates a new sense of reality in education, work, and community service. Service within the community becomes a major purpose for the adult's life. One marries, has children and establishes an environment that will best nurture them. The involvement in service continues beyond the activities of one's children and family, as one's reward becomes a major source of pleasure and joy. By age 36, this should become a sense of **self-determination**. At that time a transition will occur from "service to the community" to a "search for a philosophy of self." The search for understanding will be attained by a thorough introspection of one's beliefs and understanding of life's truth. The actions taken to learn will envelop your mind as you concentrate on discovery of your truths. As this search deepens, you will discover the essence of spiritual strength. This will result in a way to promote this concept of the newly discovered spirituality. By age 48, the mature adult should be developing an expression of **self-discipleship**. Finding the terms to give to the unseen world will be distracting, but the greater truths of your experiences will be given to **self-expression**. That expression will begin as written letters or essays for one's own understanding and then to share with others. As the importance of one's knowledge matures, you will become a teacher to small groups then later to larger groups of individuals who are seeking to share in that knowledge and revelation.

WORKBOOK CONCLUSION

Achieving the Optimum Soul Environment is everyone's goal, even if we do not consciously put this thought in these terms. Our human essence is created for us to lead to a Holy life style. Although we have forgotten this aspect of who we are and why we are, now is the time to reawaken to our greater potentials.

Every life is challenged to face hardship, endure difficulties, experience sadness, and ultimately death. Given your new awareness and enhanced consciousness you are now prepared to succeed in all matters of your life. With assurance and hope that there is meaning and purpose to life, do you now feel the courage and strength to witness to the perfection and oneness of all life? Gather the wisdom of your mental body into your physical consciousness. Bring the unconditional love of the heart body into your life. Let the freedom and beauty of your spirit body be exalted. Let your every conscious moment be understood as meaningful. **Smile**, for in all this your eternal Soul body shares and acknowledges your perfection.

Printed in the United States
1521000002B/416